THE PENGUIN POETS

D 39

ROBERT GRAVES

ROBERT GRAVES

Poems Selected by Himself

PENGUIN BOOKS

Penguin Books Ltd, Harmondsworth, Middlesex
AUSTRALIA: Penguin Books Pty Ltd, 762 Whitehorse Road,
Mitcham, Victoria

—

Published in Penguin Books 1957

Made and printed in Great Britain
by Butler & Tanner Ltd,
Frome and London

Foreword

Since these poems, written at the fairly constant rate of four or five a year since 1914, are here offered to a public considerably larger than they reached in hard-cover form, I have omitted the more baffling or shocking ones. The order is roughly chronological.

Messrs Cassell kindly allow me to make this selection from four volumes, all still available, where the remainder of my work appears:

> *Poems, 1914–1947*
> *Poems and Satires, 1951*
> *Poems, 1953*
> *The Crowning Privilege*

R. G.

Deyá, Mallorca, Spain

Contents

9

In the Wilderness

He, of his gentleness,
Thirsting and hungering
Walked in the wilderness;
Soft words of grace he spoke
Unto lost desert-folk
That listened wondering.
He heard the bittern call
From ruined palace-wall,
Answered him brotherly;
He held communion
With the she-pelican
Of lonely piety.
Basilisk, cockatrice,
Flocked to his homilies,
With mail of dread device,
With monstrous barbèd stings,
With eager dragon-eyes;
Great bats on leathern wings
And old, blind, broken things
Mean in their miseries.
Then ever with him went,
Of all his wanderings
Comrade, with ragged coat,
Gaunt ribs – poor innocent –
Bleeding foot, burning throat,
The guileless young scapegoat:
For forty nights and days
Followed in Jesus' ways,
Sure guard behind him kept,
Tears like a lover wept.

'Come, surly fellow, come: a song!'
  What, fools? Sing to you?
Choose from the clouded tales of wrong
  And terror I bring to you:

Of a night so torn with cries,
  Honest men sleeping
Start awake with rabid eyes,
  Bone-chilled, flesh creeping,

Of spirits in the web-hung room
  Up above the stable,
Groans, knocking in the gloom,
  The dancing table,

Of demons in the dry well
  That cheep and mutter,
Clanging of an unseen bell,
  Blood choking the gutter,

Of lust frightful past belief
  Lurking unforgotten,
Unrestrainable endless grief
  In breasts long rotten.

A song? What laughter or what song
  Can this house remember?
Do flowers and butterflies belong
  To a blind December?

Reproach

Your grieving moonlight face looks down
    Through the forest of my fears,
Crowned with a spiny bramble-crown,
    Bedewed with evening tears.

Why do you say 'untrue, unkind',
    Reproachful eyes that vex my sleep?
Straining in memory, I can find
    No cause why you should weep.

Untrue? But when, what broken oath?
    Unkind? I know not even your name.
Unkind, untrue, you brand me both,
    Scalding my heart with shame.

The black trees shudder, dropping snow,
    The stars tumble and spin.
Speak, speak, or how may a child know
    His ancestral sin?

The Finding of Love

Pale at first and cold,
Like wizard's lily-bloom
Conjured from the gloom,
Like torch of glow-worm seen
Through grasses shining green
By children half in fright,
Or Christmas candlelight
Flung on the outer snow,
Or tinsel stars that show
Their evening glory
With sheen of fairy story –

Now with his blaze
Love dries the cobweb maze
Dew-sagged upon the corn,
He brings the flowering thorn,
Mayfly and butterfly,
And pigeons in the sky,
Robin and thrush,
And the long bulrush,
The cherry under the leaf,
Earth in a silken dress,
With end to grief,
With joy in steadfastness.

'The General Elliot'

He fell in victory's fierce pursuit,
    Holed through and through with shot;
A sabre sweep had hacked him deep
    'Twixt neck and shoulder-knot.

The potman cannot well recall,
    The ostler never knew,
Whether that day was Malplaquet,
    The Boyne or Waterloo.

But there he hangs, a tavern sign,
    With foolish bold regard
For cock and hen and loitering men
    And wagons down the yard.

Raised high above the hayseed world
    He smokes his china pipe;
And now surveys the orchard ways,
    The damsons clustering ripe –

Stares at the churchyard slabs beyond,
    Where country neighbours lie:
Their brief renown set lowly down,
    But his invades the sky.

He grips a tankard of brown ale
    That spills a generous foam:
Often he drinks, they say, and winks
    At drunk men lurching home.

No upstart hero may usurp
    That honoured swinging seat;
His seasons pass with pipe and glass
    Until the tale's complete –

And paint shall keep his buttons bright
    Though all the world's forgot
Whether he died for England's pride
    By battle or by pot.

Rocky Acres

This is a wild land, country of my choice,
With harsh craggy mountain, moor ample and bare.
Seldom in these acres is heard any voice
But voice of cold water that runs here and there
Through rocks and lank heather growing without care.
No mice in the heath run, no song-birds fly
For fear of the buzzard that floats in the sky.

He soars and he hovers, rocking on his wings,
He scans his wide parish with a sharp eye,
He catches the trembling of small hidden things,
He tears them in pieces, dropping them from the sky;
Tenderness and pity the heart will deny,
Where life is but nourished by water and rock –
A hardy adventure, full of fear and shock.

Time has never journeyed to this lost land,
Crakeberry and heather bloom out of date,
The rocks jut, the streams flow singing on either hand,
Careless if the season be early or late,
The skies wander overhead, now blue, now slate;
Winter would be known by his cutting snow
If June did not borrow his armour also.

Yet this is my country, beloved by me best,
The first land that rose from Chaos and the Flood,
Nursing no valleys for comfort and rest,
Trampled by no shod hooves, bought with no blood.
Sempiternal country whose barrows have stood
Stronghold for demigods when on earth they go,
Terror for fat burghers on far plains below.

Outlaws

Owls – they whinny down the night;
　　Bats go zigzag by.
Ambushed in shadow beyond sight
　　The outlaws lie.

Old gods, tamed to silence, there
　　In the wet woods they lurk,
Greedy of human stuff to snare
　　In nets of murk.

Look up, else your eye will drown
　　In a moving sea of black;
Between the tree-tops, upside down,
　　Goes the sky-track.

Look up, else your feet will stray
　　Into that ambuscade
Where spider-like they trap their prey
　　With webs of shade.

For though creeds whirl away in dust,
　　Faith dies and men forget,
These agèd gods of power and lust
　　Cling to life yet –

Old gods almost dead, malign,
　　Starving for unpaid dues:
Incense and fire, salt, blood and wine
　　And a drumming muse,

Banished to woods and a sickly moon,
　　Shrunk to mere bogey things,
Who spoke with thunder once at noon
　　To prostrate kings:

With thunder from an open sky
  To warrior, virgin, priest,
Bowing in fear with a dazzled eye
  Towards the dread East –

Proud gods, humbled, sunk so low,
  Living with ghosts and ghouls,
And ghosts of ghosts and last year's snow
  And dead toadstools.

One Hard Look

Small gnats that fly
In hot July
And lodge in sleeping ears
Can rouse therein
A trumpet's din
With Day of Judgement fears.

Small mice at night
Can wake more fright
Than lions at midday;
A straw will crack
The camel's back –
There is no easier way.

One smile relieves
A heart that grieves
Though deadly sad it be,
And one hard look
Can close the book
That lovers love to see.

A Frosty Night

'Alice, dear, what ails you,
    Dazed and lost and shaken?
Has the chill night numbed you?
    Is it fright you have taken?'

'Mother, I am very well,
    I was never better.
Mother, do not hold me so,
    Let me write my letter.'

'Sweet, my dear, what ails you?'
    'No, but I am well.
The night was cold and frosty –
    There's no more to tell.'

'Ay, the night was frosty,
    Coldly gaped the moon,
Yet the birds seemed twittering
    Through green boughs of June.

'Soft and thick the snow lay,
    Stars danced in the sky –
Not all the lambs of May-day
    Skip so bold and high.

'Your feet were dancing, Alice,
    Seemed to dance on air,
You looked a ghost or angel
    In the star-light there.

'Your eyes were frosted star-light;
    Your heart, fire and snow.
Who was it said, "I love you"?'
    'Mother, let me go!'

Allie

Allie, call the birds in,
  The birds from the sky!
Allie calls, Allie sings,
  Down they all fly:
First there came
Two white doves,
  Then a sparrow from his nest,
Then a clucking bantam hen,
  Then a robin red-breast.

Allie, call the beasts in,
  The beasts, everyone!
Allie calls, Allie sings,
  In they all run:
First there came
Two black lambs,
  Then a grunting Berkshire sow,
Then a dog without a tail,
  Then a red and white cow.

Allie, call the fish up,
  The fish from the stream!
Allie calls, Allie sings,
  Up they all swim:
First there came
Two goldfish,
  A minnow and a miller's thumb,
Then a school of little trout,
  Then the twisting eels come.

Allie, call the children,
  Call them from the green!
Allie calls, Allie sings,
  Soon they run in:

First there came
Tom and Madge,
    Kate and I who'll not forget
How we played by the water's edge
    Till the April sun set.

Henry and Mary

Henry was a young king,
    Mary was his queen;
He gave her a snowdrop
    On a stalk of green.

Then all for his kindness
    And all for his care
She gave him a new-laid egg
    In the garden there.

'Love, can you sing?'
                'I cannot sing.'
  'Or tell a tale?'
              'Not one I know.'
'Then let us play at queen and king
    As down the garden walks we go.'

Love without Hope

Love without hope, as when the young bird-catcher
Swept off his tall hat to the Squire's own daughter,
So let the imprisoned larks escape and fly
Singing about her head, as she rode by.

What did I Dream?

What did I dream? I do not know –
   The fragments fly like chaff.
Yet, strange, my mind was tickled so
   I cannot help but laugh.

Pull the curtains close again,
   Tuck me grandly in;
Must a world of humour wane
   Because birds begin

Complaining in a fretful tone,
   Rousing me from sleep –
The finest entertainment known,
   And given rag-cheap?

The Country Dance

More slowly the sun travels West,
　　Earth warming beneath,
Man's heart swelling tight in his breast
　　As a bud in the sheath.

For the tender and unquiet season,
　　The Spring, drawing on
Kindles flame in the eye, chokes the reason
　　And silvers the swan.

Leap high, jealous Ralph; jet it neat,
　　Merry Jill, and remove
By employment of elbows and feet
　　The green sickness of love.

The Troll's Nosegay

A simple nosegay! was that much to ask?
(Winter still irked, with scarce a bud yet showing).
He loved her ill, if he resigned the task.
'Somewhere,' she cried, 'there must be blossom blowing.'
It seems my lady wept and the troll swore
By Heaven he hated tears: he'd cure her spleen –
Where she had begged one flower he'd shower fourscore,
A bunch fit to amaze a China Queen.

Cold fog-drawn Lily, pale mist-magic Rose
He conjured, and in a glassy cauldron set
With elvish unsubstantial Mignonette
And such vague bloom as wandering dreams enclose.
But she?
       Awed,
           Charmed to tears,
                    Distracted,
                          Yet –
Even yet, perhaps, a trifle piqued – who knows?

The Hills of May

Walking with a virgin heart
  The green hills of May,
Me, the Wind, she took as lover
  By her side to play,

Let me toss her untied hair,
  Let me shake her gown,
Careless though the daisies redden,
  Though the sun frown,

Scorning in her gay habit
  Lesser love than this,
My cool spiritual embracing,
  My secret kiss.

So she walked, the proud lady,
  So danced or ran,
So she loved with a whole heart,
  Neglecting man. . . .

Fade, fail, innocent stars
  On the green of May:
She has left our bournes for ever,
  Too fine to stay.

Lost Love

His eyes are quickened so with grief,
He can watch a grass or leaf
Every instant grow; he can
Clearly through a flint wall see,
Or watch the startled spirit flee
From the throat of a dead man.
    Across two counties he can hear
And catch your words before you speak.
The woodlouse or the maggot's weak
Clamour rings in his sad ear,
And noise so slight it would surpass
Credence – drinking sound of grass,
Worm talk, clashing jaws of moth
Chumbling holes in cloth;
The groan of ants who undertake
Gigantic loads for honour's sake
(Their sinews creak, their breath comes thin);
Whir of spiders when they spin,
And minute whispering, mumbling, sighs
Of idle grubs and flies.
    This man is quickened so with grief,
He wanders god-like or like thief
Inside and out, below, above,
Without relief seeking lost love.

Vain and Careless

Lady, lovely lady,
   Careless and gay!
Once, when a beggar called,
   She gave her child away.

The beggar took the baby,
   Wrapped it in a shawl –
'Bring him back,' the lady said,
   'Next time you call.'

Hard by lived a vain man,
   So vain and so proud
He would walk on stilts
   To be seen by the crowd,

Up above the chimney pots,
   Tall as a mast –
And all the people ran about
   Shouting till he passed.

'A splendid match surely,'
   Neighbours saw it plain,
'Although she is so careless,
   Although he is so vain.'

But the lady played bobcherry,
   Did not see or care,
As the vain man went by her,
   Aloft in the air.

This gentle-born couple
   Lived and died apart –
Water will not mix with oil,
   Nor vain with careless heart.

An English Wood

This valley wood is pledged
To the set shape of things,
And reasonably hedged:
Here are no harpies fledged,
No rocs may clap their wings,
Nor gryphons wave their stings.
Here, poised in quietude,
Calm elementals brood
On the set shape of things:
They fend away alarms
From this green wood.
Here nothing is that harms –
No bulls with lungs of brass,
No toothed or spiny grass,
No tree whose clutching arms
Drink blood when travellers pass,
No mount of glass;
No bardic tongues unfold
Satires or charms.
Only, the lawns are soft,
The tree-stems, grave and old;
Slow branches sway aloft,
The evening air comes cold,
The sunset scatters gold.
Small grasses toss and bend,
Small pathways idly tend
Towards no fearful end.

The Bedpost

Sleepy Betsy from her pillow
   Sees the post and ball
Of her sister's wooden bedstead
   Shadowed on the wall.

Now this grave young warrior standing
   With uncovered head
Tells her stories of old battle
   As she lies in bed:

How the Emperor and the Farmer,
   Fighting knee to knee,
Broke their swords but whirled their scabbards
   Till they gained the sea.

How the ruler of that shore
   Foully broke his oath,
Gave them beds in his sea cave,
   Then stabbed them both.

How the daughters of the Emperor,
   Diving boldly through
Caught and killed their father's murderer,
   Old Cro-bar-cru.

How the Farmer's sturdy sons
   Fought the Giant Gog,
Threw him into Stony Cataract
   In the land of Og.

Will and Abel were their names,
   Though they went by others:
He could tell ten thousand stories
   Of these lusty brothers.

How the Emperor's elder daughter
　　Fell in love with Will
And went with him to the Court of Venus
　　Over Hoo Hill;

How Gog's wife encountered Abel
　　Whom she hated most,
Stole away his arms and helmet,
　　Turned him to a post.

As a post he shall stay rooted
　　For yet many years,
Until a maiden shall release him
　　With pitying tears.

But Betsy likes the bloodier stories,
　　Clang and clash of fight,
And Abel wanes with the spent candle –
　　'Sweetheart, good-night!'

The Pier-Glass

Lost manor where I walk continually
A ghost, though yet in woman's flesh and blood:
Up your broad stairs mounting with outspread fingers
And gliding steadfast down your corridors
I come by nightly custom to this room,
And even on sultry afternoons I come
Drawn by a thread of time-sunk memory.

Empty, unless for a huge bed of state
Shrouded with rusty curtains drooped awry
(A puppet theatre where malignant fancy
Peoples the wings with fear). At my right hand
A ravelled bell-pull hangs in readiness
To summon me from attic glooms above
Service of elder ghosts; here, at my left,
A sullen pier-glass, cracked from side to side,
Scorns to present the face (as do new mirrors)
With a lying flush, but shows it melancholy
And pale, as faces grow that look in mirrors.

Is there no life, nothing but the thin shadow
And blank foreboding, never a wainscot rat
Rasping a crust? Or at the window-pane
No fly, no bluebottle, no starveling spider?
The windows frame a prospect of cold skies
Half-merged with sea, as at the first creation –
Abstract, confusing welter. Face about,
Peer rather in the glass once more, take note
Of self, the grey lips and long hair dishevelled,
Sleep-staring eyes. Ah, mirror, for Christ's love
Give me one token that there still abides
Remote – beyond this island mystery,
So be it only this side Hope, somewhere,
In streams, on sun-warm mountain pasturage –
True life, natural breath; not this phantasma.

Apples and Water

Dust in a cloud, blinding weather,
   Drums that rattle and roar!
A mother and daughter stood together
   By their cottage door.

'Mother, the heavens are bright like brass,
   The dust is shaken high,
With labouring breath the soldiers pass,
   Their lips are cracked and dry.

'Mother, I'll throw them apples down,
   I'll fetch them cups of water.'
The mother turned with an angry frown,
   Holding back her daughter.

'But, mother, see, they faint with thirst,
   They march away to war.'
'Ay, daughter, these are not the first
   And there will come yet more.

'There is no water can supply them
   In western streams that flow;
There is no fruit can satisfy them
   On orchard-trees that grow.

'Once in my youth I gave, poor fool,
   A soldier apples and water;
And may I die before you cool
   Such drouth as his, my daughter.'

Angry Samson

Are they blind, the lords of Gaza
   In their strong towers,
Who declare Samson pillow-smothered
   And stripped of his powers?

O stolid Philistines,
   Stare now in amaze
At my foxes running in your cornfields
   With their tails ablaze,

At swung jaw-bone, at bees swarming
   In the stark lion's hide,
At these, the gates of well-walled Gaza
   A-clank to my stride.

Down

Downstairs a clock had chimed, two o'clock only.
Then outside from the hen-roost crowing came.
Why should the shift-wing call against the clock,
Three hours from dawn? Now shutters click and knock,
And he remembers a sad superstition
Unfitting for the sick-bed. . . . Turn aside,
Distract, divide, ponder the simple tales
That puzzled childhood; riddles, turn them over –
Half-riddles, answerless, the more intense.
Lost bars of music tinkling with no sense
Recur, drowning uneasy superstition.

Mouth open, he was lying, this sick man,
And sinking all the while; how had he come
To sink? On better nights his dream went flying,
Dipping, sailing the pasture of his sleep,
But now (since clock and cock) had sunk him down
Through mattress, bed, floor, floors beneath, stairs, cellars,
Through deep foundations of the manse; still sinking
Through unturned earth. How had he magicked space
With inadvertent motion or word uttered
Of too-close-packed intelligence (such there are),
That he should penetrate with sliding ease
Dense earth, compound of ages, granite ribs
And groins? Consider: there was some word uttered,
Some abracadabra – then, like a stage-ghost,
Funereally with weeping, down, drowned, lost!

Oh, to be a child once more, sprawling at ease
On smooth turf of a ruined castle court.
Once he had dropped a stone between the slabs
That masked an ancient well, mysteriously
Plunging his mind down with it. Hear it go

Rattling and rocketing into secret void!
Count slowly: one, two, three! and echoes come
Fainter and fainter, merged in the general hum
Of bees and flies; only a thin draught rises
To chill the drowsy air. There he had lain
As if unborn, until life floated back
From the deep waters.

     Oh, to renew now
That bliss of repossession, kindly sun
Forfeit for ever, and the towering sky.

Falling, falling! Day closed up behind him.
Now stunned by the violent subterrene flow
Of rivers, whirling down to hiss below
On the flame-axis of this terrible earth;
Toppling upon their waterfall, O spirit. . . .

Mermaid, Dragon, Fiend

In my childhood rumours ran
    Of a world beyond our door –
Terrors to the life of man
    That the highroad held in store.

Of the mermaids' doleful game
    In deep water I heard tell,
Of lofty dragons belching flame,
    Of the hornèd fiend of Hell.

Tales like these were too absurd
    For my laughter-loving ear:
Soon I mocked at all I heard,
    Though with cause indeed for fear.

Now I know the mermaid kin
    I find them bound by natural laws:
They have neither tail nor fin,
    But are deadlier for that cause.

Dragons have no darting tongues,
    Teeth saw-edged nor rattling scales,
No fire issues from their lungs,
    No black poison from their tails:

For they are creatures of dark air,
    Unsubstantial tossing forms,
Thunderclaps of man's despair
    In mid-whirl of mental storms.

And there's a true and only fiend
    Worse than prophets prophesy,
Whose full powers to hurt are screened
    Lest the race of man should die.

Ever in vain will courage plot
   The dragon's death, in coat of proof;
Or love abjure the mermaid grot;
   Or faith denounce the cloven hoof.

Mermaids will not be denied
   The last bubbles of our shame,
The dragon flaunts an unpierced hide,
   The true fiend governs in God's name.

In Procession

Often, half-way to sleep,
Not yet sunken deep –
The sudden moment on me comes
From a mountain shagged and steep,
With terrible roll of dream drums,
Reverberations, cymbals, horns replying.
When with standards flying,
Horsemen in clouds behind,
The coloured pomps unwind,
The Carnival wagons
With their saints and their dragons
On the scroll of my teeming mind:
The Creation and Flood
With our Saviour's Blood
And fat Silenus' flagons,
And every rare beast
From the South and East,
Both greatest and least,
On and on,
In endless, variant procession.
I stand at the top rungs
Of a ladder reared in the air,
And I rail in strange tongues,
So the crowds murmur and stare;
Then volleys again the blare
Of horns, and summer flowers
Fly scattering in showers,
And the sun leaps in the sky,
While the drums thumping by
Proclaim me. . . .
Oh, then, when I wake,
Could I courage take
To renew my speech,

Could I stretch and reach
The flowers and the ripe fruit
Laid out at the ladder's foot,
Could I rip a silken shred
From the banner tossed ahead,
Could I call a double-flam
From the drums, could the goat
Horned with gold, could the ram
With a flank like a barn-door,
The dwarf, the blackamoor,
Could Jonah and the Whale
And the Holy Grail,
The Ape with his platter
Going clitter-clatter,
The Nymphs and the Satyr,
And every marvellous matter
Come before me here,
Standing near and clear –
Could I make it so that you
Might wonder at them too!
– Glories of land and sea,
Of Heaven glittering free,
Castles hugely built in Spain,
Glories of Cockaigne,
Of that spicy kingdom, Cand,
Of the Delectable Land,
Of the Land of Crooked Stiles,
Of the Fortunate Isles,
Of the more than three-score miles
That to Babylon lead
(A pretty city indeed
Built on a four-square plan),
Of the Land of the Gold Man
Whose eager horses whinny
In their cribs of gold,

Of the Land of Whipperginny,
Of the land where none grows old. . . .
But cowardly I tell,
Rather, of the Town of Hell –
A huddle of dirty woes
And houses in fading rows
Straggled through space:
Hell has no market-place,
Nor point where four ways meet,
Nor principal street,
Nor barracks, nor Town Hall,
Nor shops at all,
Nor rest for weary feet,
Nor theatre, square, or park,
Nor lights after dark,
Nor churches, nor inns,
Nor convenience for sins –
Neither ends nor begins,
Rambling, limitless, hated well,
This Town of Hell
Where between sleep and sleep I dwell.

Warning to Children

Children, if you dare to think
Of the greatness, rareness, muchness,
Fewness of this precious only
Endless world in which you say
You live, you think of things like this:
Blocks of slate enclosing dappled
Red and green, enclosing tawny
Yellow nets, enclosing white
And black acres of dominoes,
Where a neat brown paper parcel
Tempts you to untie the string.
In the parcel a small island,
On the island a large tree,
On the tree a husky fruit.
Strip the husk and pare the rind off:
In the kernel you will see
Blocks of slate enclosed by dappled
Red and green, enclosed by tawny
Yellow nets, enclosed by white
And black acres of dominoes,
Where the same brown paper parcel –
Children, leave the string untied!
For who dares undo the parcel
Finds himself at once inside it,
On the island, in the fruit,
Blocks of slate about his head,
Finds himself enclosed by dappled
Green and red, enclosed by yellow
Tawny nets, enclosed by black
And white acres of dominoes,
With the same brown paper parcel
Still untied upon his knee.

And, if he then should dare to think
Of the fewness, muchness, rareness,
Greatness of this endless only
Precious world in which he says
He lives – he then unties the string.

Alice

When that prime heroine of our nation, Alice,
Climbing courageously in through the Palace
Of Looking Glass, found it inhabited
By chessboard personages, white and red,
Involved in never-ending tournament,
She being of a speculative bent
Had long foreshadowed something of the kind,
Asking herself: 'Suppose I stood behind
And viewed the fireplace of Their drawing-room
From hearthrug level, why must I assume
That what I'd see would need to correspond
With what I now see? And the rooms beyond?'

Proved right, yet not content with what she had done,
Alice decided to increase her fun:
She set herself, with truly British pride
In being a pawn and playing for her side,
And simple faith in simple stratagem,
To learn the rules and moves and perfect them.
So prosperously there she settled down
That six moves only and she'd won her crown –
A triumph surely! But her greater feat
Was rounding these adventures off complete:
Accepting them, when safe returned again,
As queer but true, not only in the main
True, but as true as anything you'd swear to,
The usual three dimensions you are heir to.
For Alice though a child could understand
That neither did this chance-discovered land
Make nohow or contrariwise the clean
Dull round of mid-Victorian routine,
Nor did Victoria's golden rule extend
Beyond the glass: it came to the dead end

Where empty hearses turn about; thereafter
Begins that lubberland of dream and laughter,
The red-and-white-flower-spangled hedge, the grass
Where Apuleius pastured his Gold Ass,
Where young Gargantua made whole holiday . . .
But further from our heroine not to stray,
Let us observe with what uncommon sense –
Though a secure and easy reference
Between Red Queen and Kitten could be found –
She made no false assumption on that ground
(A trap in which the scientist would fall)
That queens and kittens are identical.

Ancestors

My New Year's drink is mulled to-night
    And hot sweet vapours roofward twine.
The shades cry *Gloria!* with delight
    As down they troop to taste old wine.

They crowd about the crackling fire,
    Impatient as the rites begin;
Mulled porto is their souls' desire –
    Porto well aged with nutmeg in.

'Ha,' cries the first, 'my Alma wine
    Of one-and-seventy years ago!'
The second cheers 'God bless the vine!'
    The third and fourth like cockerels crow:

They crow and clap their arms for wings,
    They have small pride or breeding left –
Two grey-beards, a tall youth who sings,
    A soldier with his cheek-bone cleft.

O *Gloria!* for each ghostly shape,
    That whiffled like a candle smoke,
Now fixed and ruddy with the grape
    And mirrored at the polished oak.

I watch their brightening boastful eyes,
    I hear the toast their glasses clink:
'May this young man in drink grown wise
    Die, as we also died, in drink!'

Their reedy voices I abhor,
    I am alive at least, and young.
I dash their swill upon the floor:
    Let them lap grovelling, tongue to tongue.

The Cool Web

Children are dumb to say how hot the day is,
How hot the scent is of the summer rose,
How dreadful the black wastes of evening sky,
How dreadful the tall soldiers drumming by.

But we have speech, to chill the angry day,
And speech, to dull the rose's cruel scent.
We spell away the overhanging night,
We spell away the soldiers and the fright.

There's a cool web of language winds us in,
Retreat from too much joy or too much fear:
We grow sea-green at last and coldly die
In brininess and volubility.

But if we let our tongues lose self-possession,
Throwing off language and its watery clasp
Before our death, instead of when death comes,
Facing the wide glare of the children's day,
Facing the rose, the dark sky and the drums,
We shall go mad no doubt and die that way.

Love in Barrenness

Below the ridge a raven flew
And we heard the lost curlew
Mourning out of sight below.
Mountain tops were touched with snow;
Even the long dividing plain
Showed no wealth of sheep or grain,
But fields of boulders lay like corn
And raven's croak was shepherd's horn
Where slow cloud-shadow strayed across
A pasture of thin heath and moss.

The North Wind rose: I saw him press
With lusty force against your dress,
Moulding your body's inward grace
And streaming off from your set face;
So now no longer flesh and blood
But poised in marble flight you stood.
O wingless Victory, loved of men,
Who could withstand your beauty then?

Song of Contrariety

Far away is close at hand,
Close joined is far away,
Love shall come at your command
Yet will not stay.

At summons of your dream-despair
She might not disobey,
But slid close down beside you there,
And complaisant lay.

Yet now her flesh and blood consent
In the hours of day,
Joy and passion both are spent,
Twining clean away.

Is the person empty air,
Is the spectre clay
That love, lent substance by despair,
Wanes and leaves you lonely there
On the bridal day?

The Presence

Why say 'death'? Death is neither harsh nor kind:
Other pleasures or pains could hold the mind
If she were dead. For dead is gone indeed,
Lost beyond recovery and need,
Discarded, ended, rotted underground –
Of whom no personal feature could be found
To stand out from the soft blur evenly spread
On memory, if she were truly dead.

But living still, barred from accustomed use
Of body and dress and motion, with profuse
Reproaches (since this anguish of her grew
Do I still love her as I swear I do?)
She fills the house and garden terribly
With her bewilderment, accusing me,
Till every stone and flower, table and book,
Cries out her name, pierces me with her look,
'You are deaf, listen!
You are blind, see!'
                How deaf or blind,
When horror of the grave maddens the mind
With those same pangs that lately choked her breath,
Altered her substance, and made sport of death?

The Land of Whipperginny

Come closer yet, my honeysuckle, my sweetheart Jinny:
  A low sun is gilding the bloom of the wood –
Is it Heaven, or Hell, or the Land of Whipperginny
  That holds this fairy lustre, not yet understood?

For stern proud psalms from the chapel on the moors
  Waver in the night wind, their firm rhythm broken,
Lugubriously twisted to a howling of whores
  Or lent an airy glory too strange to be spoken.

Soon the risen Moon will peer down with pity,
  Drawing us in secret by an ivory gate
To the fruit-plats and fountains of her silver city
  Where lovers need not argue the tokens of fate.

In No Direction

To go in no direction
  Surely as carelessly,
Walking on the hills alone,
  I never found easy.

Either I sent leaf or stick
  Twirling in the air,
Whose fall might be prophetic,
  Pointing 'there',

Or in superstition
  Edged somewhat away
From a sure direction,
  Yet could not stray,

Or undertook the climb
  That I had avoided
Directionless some other time,
  Or had not avoided,

Or called as companion
  Some eyeglass ghost
And held his no direction
  Till my feet were lost.

The Castle

Walls, mounds, enclosing corrugations
Of darkness, moonlight on dry grass.
Walking this courtyard, sleepless, in fever;
Planning to use – but by definition
There's no way out, no way out –
Rope-ladders, baulks of timber, pulleys,
A rocket whizzing over the walls and moat –
Machines easy to improvise.
                          No escape,
No such thing; to dream of new dimensions,
Cheating checkmate by painting the king's robe
So that he slides like a queen;
Or to cry, 'Nightmare, nightmare!'
Like a corpse in the cholera-pit
Under a load of corpses;
Or to run the head against these blind walls,
Enter the dungeon, torment the eyes
With apparitions chained two and two,
And go frantic with fear –
To die and wake up sweating by moonlight
In the same courtyard, sleepless as before.

Return

The seven years' curse is ended now
That drove me forth from this kind land,
From mulberry-bough and apple-bough
And gummy twigs the west wind shakes,
To drink the brine from crusted lakes
And grit my teeth on sand.

Now for your cold, malicious brain
And most uncharitable, cold heart,
You, too, shall clank the seven years' chain
On sterile ground for all time cursed
With famine's itch and flames of thirst,
The blank sky's counterpart.

The load that from my shoulder slips
Straightway upon your own is tied:
You, too, shall scorch your finger-tips
With scrabbling on the desert's face
Such thoughts I had of this green place,
Sent scapegoat for your pride.

Here, Robin on a tussock sits,
And Cuckoo with his call of hope
Cuckoos awhile, then off he flits,
While peals of dingle-dongle keep
Troop-discipline among the sheep
That graze across the slope.

A brook from fields of gentle sun,
Through the glade its water heaves,
The falling cone would well-nigh stun
That Squirrel wantonly lets drop
When up he scampers to tree-top
And dives among the green.

But no, I ask a surer peace
Than vengeance on you could provide.
Then fear no ill from my release:
Be off, elude the curse, disgrace
Some other green and happy place –
This world of fools is wide.

The Bards

The bards falter in shame, their running verse
Stumbles, with marrow-bones the drunken diners
Pelt them for their delay.
It is a something fearful in the song
Plagues them – an unknown grief that like a churl
Goes commonplace in cowskin
And bursts unheralded, crowing and coughing,
An unpilled holly-club twirled in his hand,
Into their many-shielded, samite-curtained,
Jewel-bright hall where twelve kings sit at chess
Over the white-bronze pieces and the gold;
And by a gross enchantment
Flails down the rafters and leads off the queens –
The wild-swan-breasted, the rose-ruddy-cheeked
Raven-haired daughters of their admiration –
To stir his black pots and to bed on straw.

Nobody

Nobody, ancient mischief, nobody,
Harasses always with an absent body.

Nobody coming up the road, nobody,
Like a tall man in a dark cloak, nobody.

Nobody about the house, nobody,
Like children creeping up the stairs, nobody.

Nobody anywhere in the garden, nobody,
Like a young girl quiet with needlework, nobody.

Nobody coming, nobody, not yet here,
Incessantly welcomed by the wakeful ear.

Until this nobody shall consent to die
Under his curse must everybody lie –

The curse of his envy, of his grief and fright,
Of sudden rape and murder screamed in the night.

Full Moon

As I walked out that sultry night,
    I heard the stroke of one.
The moon, attained to her full height,
    Stood beaming like the sun:
She exorcized the ghostly wheat
To mute assent in love's defeat,
    Whose tryst had now begun.

The fields lay sick beneath my tread,
    A tedious owlet cried,
A nightingale above my head
    With this or that replied –
Like man and wife who nightly keep
Inconsequent debate in sleep
    As they dream side by side.

Your phantom wore the moon's cold mask,
    My phantom wore the same;
Forgetful of the feverish task
    In hope of which they came,
Each image held the other's eyes
And watched a grey distraction rise
    To cloud the eager flame –

To cloud the eager flame of love,
    To fog the shining gate;
They held the tyrannous queen above
    Sole mover of their fate,
They glared as marble statues glare
Across the tessellated stair
    Or down the halls of state.

And now warm earth was Arctic sea,
    Each breath came dagger-keen;

Two bergs of glinting ice were we,
    The broad moon sailed between;
There swam the mermaids, tailed and finned,
And love went by upon the wind
    As though it had not been.

Be assured, the Dragon is not dead
But once more from the pools of peace
Shall rear his fabulous green head.

The flowers of innocence shall cease
And like a harp the wind shall roar
And the clouds shake an angry fleece.

'Here, here is certitude,' you swore,
'Below this lightning-blasted tree.
Where once it strikes, it strikes no more.

'Two lovers in one house agree.
The roof is tight, the walls unshaken.
As now, so must it always be.'

Such prophecies of joy awaken
The toad who dreams away the past
Under your hearth-stone, light forsaken,

Who knows that certitude at last
Must melt away in vanity –
No gate is fast, no door is fast –

That thunder bursts from the blue sky,
That gardens of the mind fall waste,
That fountains of the heart run dry.

Pure Death

We looked, we loved, and therewith instantly
Death became terrible to you and me.
By love we disenthralled our natural terror
From every comfortable philosopher
Or tall, grey doctor of divinity:
Death stood at last in his true rank and order.

It happened soon, so wild of heart were we,
Exchange of gifts grew to a malady:
Their worth rose always higher on each side
Till there seemed nothing but ungivable pride
That yet remained ungiven, and this degree
Called a conclusion not to be denied.

Then we at last bethought ourselves, made shift
And simultaneously this final gift
Gave: each with shaking hands unlocks
The sinister, long, brass-bound coffin-box,
Unwraps pure death, with such bewilderment
As greeted our love's first acknowledgement.

Sick Love

O Love, be fed with apples while you may,
And feel the sun and go in royal array,
A smiling innocent on the heavenly causeway,

Though in what listening horror for the cry
That soars in outer blackness dismally,
The dumb blind beast, the paranoiac fury:

Be warm, enjoy the season, lift your head,
Exquisite in the pulse of tainted blood,
That shivering glory not to be despised.

Take your delight in momentariness,
Walk between dark and dark – a shining space
With the grave's narrowness, though not its peace.

It Was All Very Tidy

When I reached his place,
The grass was smooth,
The wind was delicate,
The wit well timed,
The limbs well formed,
The pictures straight on the wall:
It was all very tidy.

He was cancelling out
The last row of figures,
He had his beard tied up in ribbons,
There was no dust on his shoe,
Everyone nodded:
It was all very tidy.

Music was not playing,
There were no sudden noises,
The sun shone blandly,
The clock ticked:
It was all very tidy.

'Apart from and above all this,'
I reassured myself,
'There is now myself.'
It was all very tidy.

Death did not address me,
He had nearly done:
It was all very tidy.

They asked, did I not think
It was all very tidy?

I could not bring myself
To laugh, or untie

His beard's neat ribbons,
Or jog his elbow,
Or whistle, or sing,
Or make disturbance.
I consented, frozenly,
He was unexceptionable:
It was all very tidy.

Thief

To the galleys, thief, and sweat your soul out
With strong tugging under the curled whips,
That there your thievishness may find full play.
Whereas, before, you stole rings, flowers and watches,
Oaths, jests and proverbs,
Yet paid for bed and board like an honest man,
This shall be entire thiefdom: you shall steal
Sleep from chain-galling, diet from sour crusts,
Comradeship from the damned, the ten-year-chained –
And, more than this, the excuse for life itself
From a craft steered toward battles not your own.

The Furious Voyage

So, overmasterful, to sea!
But hope no distant view of sail,
No growling ice, nor weed, nor whale,
Nor breakers perilous on the lee.

Though you enlarge your angry mind
Three leagues and more about the ship
And stamp till every puncheon skip,
The wake runs evenly behind.

And it has width enough for you,
This vessel, dead from truck to keel,
With its unmanageable wheel,
Its blank chart and the surly crew,

In ballast only due to fetch
The turning point of wretchedness
On an uncoasted, featureless
And barren ocean of blue stretch.

Song: Lift-Boy

Let me tell you the story of how I began:
I began as the knife-boy and ended as the boot-man,
With nothing in my pockets but a jack-knife and a button,
With nothing in my pockets but a jack-knife and a button,
With nothing in my pockets.

Let me tell you the story of how I went on:
I began as the lift-boy and ended as the lift-man,
With nothing in my pockets but a jack-knife and a button,
With nothing in my pockets but a jack-knife and a button,
With nothing in my pockets.

I found it very easy to whistle and play
With nothing in my head or my pockets all day,
With nothing in my pockets.

But along came Old Eagle, like Moses or David,
He stopped at the fourth floor and preached me Damnation:
'Not a soul shall be savèd, not one shall be savèd.
The whole First Creation shall forfeit salvation:
From knife-boy to lift-boy, from ragged to regal,
Not one shall be savèd, not you, not Old Eagle,
No soul on earth escapeth, even if all repent –'
So I cut the cords of the lift and down we went,
With nothing in our pockets.

Ulysses

To the much-tossed Ulysses, never done
  With woman whether gowned as wife or whore,
Penelope and Circe seemed as one:
She like a whore made his lewd fancies run,
  And wifely she a hero to him bore.

Their counter-changings terrified his way:
  They were the clashing rocks, Symplegades,
Scylla and Charybdis too were they;
Now they were storms frosting the sea with spray
  And now the lotus island's drunken ease.

They multiplied into the Sirens' throng,
  Forewarned by fear of whom he stood bound fast
Hand and foot helpless to the vessel's mast,
Yet would not stop his ears: daring their song
  He groaned and sweated till that shore was past.

One, two and many: flesh had made him blind,
  Flesh had one pleasure only in the act,
Flesh set one purpose only in the mind –
Triumph of flesh and afterwards to find
  Still those same terrors wherewith flesh was racked.

His wiles were witty and his fame far known,
Every king's daughter sought him for her own,
  Yet he was nothing to be won or lost.
  All lands to him were Ithaca: love-tossed
He loathed the fraud, yet would not bed alone.

The Succubus

Thus will despair
In ecstasy of nightmare
Fetch you a devil-woman through the air,
  To slide below the sweated sheet
And kiss your lips in answer to your prayer
  And lock her hands with yours and your feet with her feet.

Yet why does she
Come never as longed-for beauty
Slender and cool, with limbs lovely to see,
  (The bedside candle guttering high)
And toss her head so the thick curls fall free
  Of halo'd breast, firm belly and long, slender thigh?

Why with hot face,
With paunched and uddered carcase,
Sudden and greedily does she embrace,
  Gulping away your soul, she lies so close,
Fathering you with brats of her own race?
  Yet is the fancy grosser than your lusts were gross?

The Reader over My Shoulder

You reading over my shoulder, peering beneath
My writing arm – I suddenly feel your breath
Hot on my hand or on my nape,
So interrupt my theme, scratching these few
Words on the margin for you, namely you,
Too-human shape fixed in that shape: –

All the saying of things against myself
And for myself I have well done myself.
What now, old enemy, shall you do
But quote and underline, thrusting yourself
Against me, as ambassador of myself,
In damned confusion of myself and you?

For you in strutting, you in sycophancy,
Have played too long this other self of me,
Doubling the part of judge and patron
With that of creaking grind-stone to my wit.
Know me, have done: I am a proud spirit
And you for ever clay. Have done.

The Legs

There was this road,
And it led up-hill,
And it led down-hill,
And round and in and out.

And the traffic was legs,
Legs from the knees down,
Coming and going,
Never pausing.

And the gutters gurgled
With the rain's overflow,
And the sticks on the pavement
Blindly tapped and tapped.

What drew the legs along
Was the never-stopping,
And the senseless, frightening
Fate of being legs.

Legs for the road,
The road for legs,
Resolutely nowhere
In both directions.

My legs at least
Were not in that rout:
On grass by the road-side
Entire I stood,

Watching the unstoppable
Legs go by
With never a stumble
Between step and step.

Though my smile was broad
The legs could not see,
Though my laugh was loud
The legs could not hear.

My head dizzied, then:
I wondered suddenly,
Might I too be a walker
From the knees down?

Gently I touched my shins.
The doubt unchained them:
They had run in twenty puddles
Before I regained them.

Gardener

Loveliest flowers, though crooked in their border,
And glorious fruit, dangled from ill-pruned boughs –
Be sure the gardener had not eye enough
To wheel a barrow between the broadest gates
Without a clumsy scraping.

Yet none could think it simple awkwardness;
And when he stammered of a garden-guardian,
That the smooth lawns came by angelic favour,
The pinks and pears in spite of his own blunders,
They nudged at this conceit.

Well, he had something, though he called it nothing –
An ass's wit, a hairy-belly shrewdness
That would appraise the intentions of the angel
By the very difference of his own confusion,
And bring the most to pass.

In Broken Images

He is quick, thinking in clear images;
I am slow, thinking in broken images.

He becomes dull, trusting to his clear images;
I become sharp, mistrusting my broken images.

Trusting his images, he assumes their relevance;
Mistrusting my images, I question their relevance.

Assuming their relevance, he assumes the fact;
Questioning their relevance, I question the fact.

When the fact fails him, he questions his senses;
When the fact fails me, I approve my senses.

He continues quick and dull in his clear images;
I continue slow and sharp in my broken images.

He in a new confusion of his understanding;
I in a new understanding of my confusion.

On Rising Early

Rising early and walking in the garden
Before the sun has properly climbed the hill –
His rays warming the roof, not yet the grass
That is white with dew still.

And not enough breeze to eddy a puff of smoke,
And out in the meadows a thick mist lying yet,
And nothing anywhere ill or noticeable –
Thanks indeed for that.

But was there ever a day with wit enough
To be always early, to draw the smoke up straight
Even at three o'clock of an afternoon,
To spare dullness or sweat?

Indeed, many such days I remember
That were dew-white and gracious to the last,
That ruled out meal-times, yet had no more hunger
Than was felt by rising a half-hour before breakfast,
Nor more fatigue – where was it that I went
So unencumbered, with my feet trampling
Like strangers on the past?

Flying Crooked

The butterfly, a cabbage-white,
(His honest idiocy of flight)
Will never now, it is too late,
Master the art of flying straight,
Yet has – who knows so well as I? –
A just sense of how not to fly:
He lurches here and here by guess
And God and hope and hopelessness.
Even the aerobatic swift
Has not his flying-crooked gift.

Fragment of a Lost Poem

O the clear moment, when from the mouth
A word flies, current immediately
Among friends; or when a loving gift astounds
As the identical wish nearest the heart;
Or when a stone, volleyed in sudden danger,
Strikes the rabid beast full on the snout!

Moments in never. . . .

The Devil's Advice to Story-Tellers

Lest men suspect your tale to be untrue,
Keep probability – some say – in view.
But my advice to story-tellers is:
Weigh out no gross of probabilities,
Nor yet make diligent transcriptions of
Known instances of virtue, crime or love.
To forge a picture that will pass for true,
Do conscientiously what liars do –
Born liars, not the lesser sort that raid
The mouths of others for their stock-in-trade:
Assemble, first, all casual bits and scraps
That may shake down into a world perhaps;
People this world, by chance created so,
With random persons whom you do not know –
The teashop sort, or travellers in a train
Seen once, guessed idly at, not seen again;
Let the erratic course they steer surprise
Their own and your own and your readers' eyes;
Sigh then, or frown, but leave (as in despair)
Motive and end and moral in the air;
Nice contradiction between fact and fact
Will make the whole read human and exact.

Into a gentle wilderness and confusion,
Of here and there, of one and everyone,
Of windy sandhills by an unkempt sea,
Came two and two in search of symmetry,
Found symmetry of two in sea and sand,
In left foot, right foot, left hand and right hand.

The beast with two backs is a single beast,
Yet by his love of singleness increased
To two and two and two and two again,
Until, instead of sandhills, see, a plain
Patterned in two and two, by two and two –
And the sea parts in horror at a view
Of rows of houses coupling, back to back,
While love smokes from their common chimney-stack
With two-four-eight-sixteenish single same
Re-registration of the duple name.

Wm. Brazier

At the end of Tarriers' Lane, which was the street
We children thought the pleasantest in Town
Because of the old elms growing from the pavement
And the crookedness, when the other streets were straight,
[They were always at the lamp-post round the corner,
Those pugs and papillons and in-betweens,
Nosing and snuffling for the latest news]
Lived Wm. Brazier, with a gilded sign,
'Practical Chimney Sweep.' He had black hands,
Black face, black clothes, black brushes and white teeth;
He jingled round the town in a pony-trap,
And the pony's name was Soot, and Soot was black.
But the brass fittings on the trap, the shafts,
On Soot's black harness, on the black whip-butt,
Twinkled and shone like any guardsman's buttons.
Wasn't that pretty? And when we children jeered:
'Hello, Wm. Brazier! Dirty-face Wm. Brazier!'
He would crack his whip at us and smile and bellow,
'Hello, my dears!' [If he were drunk, but otherwise:
'Scum off, you damned young milliners' bastards, you!']

Let them copy it out on a pink page of their albums,
Carefully leaving out the bracketed lines.
It's an old story – f's for s's –
But good enough for them, the suckers.

'But that was nothing to what things came out
From the sea-caves of Criccieth yonder.'
'What were they? Mermaids? dragons? ghosts?'
'Nothing at all of any things like that.'
'What were they, then?'
                              'All sorts of queer things,
Things never seen or heard or written about,
Very strange, un-Welsh, utterly peculiar
Things. Oh, solid enough they seemed to touch,
Had anyone dared it. Marvellous creation,
All various shapes and sizes and no sizes,
All new, each perfectly unlike his neighbour,
Though all came moving slowly out together.'
'Describe just one of them.'
                              'I am unable.'
'What were their colours?'
                              'Mostly nameless colours,
Colours you'd like to see; but one was puce
Or perhaps more like crimson, but not purplish.
Some had no colour.'
                    'Tell me, had they legs?'
'Not a leg nor foot among them that I saw.'
'But did these things come out in any order?
What o'clock was it? What was the day of the week?
Who else was present? How was the weather?'
'I was coming to that. It was half-past three
On Easter Tuesday last. The sun was shining.
The Harlech Silver Band played *Marchog Jesu*
On thirty-seven shimmering instruments,
Collecting for Carnarvon's (Fever) Hospital Fund.
The populations of Pwllheli, Criccieth,
Portmadoc, Borth, Tremadoc, Penrhyndeudraeth,
Were all assembled. Criccieth's mayor addressed them

First in good Welsh and then in fluent English,
Twisting his fingers in his chain of office,
Welcoming the things. They came out on the sand,
Not keeping time to the band, moving seaward
Silently at a snail's pace. But at last
The most odd, indescribable thing of all,
Which hardly one man there could see for wonder
Did something recognizably a something.'
'Well, what?'
                    'It made a noise.'
                              'A frightening noise?'
'No, no.'
          'A musical noise? A noise of scuffling?'
'No, but a very loud, respectable noise –
Like groaning to oneself on Sunday morning
In Chapel, close before the second psalm.'
'What did the mayor do?'
                              'I was coming to that.'

Hell

Husks, rags and bones, waste-paper, excrement,
   Denied a soul whether for good or evil
And casually consigned to unfulfilment,
   Are pronged into his bag by the great-devil.

Or words repeated, over and over and over,
   Until their sense sickens and all but dies,
These the same fellow like a ghoulish lover
   Will lay his hands upon and hypnotize.

From husks and rags and waste and excrement
   He forms the pavement-feet and the lift-faces;
He steers the sick words into parliament
   To rule a dust-bin world with deep-sleep phrases.

When healthy words or people chance to dine
   Together in this rarely actual scene,
There is a love-taste in the bread and wine,
   Nor is it asked: 'Do you mean what you mean?'

But to their table-converse boldly comes
   The same great-devil with his brush and tray,
To conjure plump loaves from the scattered crumbs,
   And feed his false five thousands day by day.

Synthetic Such

'The sum of all the parts of Such –
    Of each laboratory scene –
Is Such.' While Science means this much
    And means no more, why, let it mean!

But were the science-men to find
    Some animating principle
Which gave synthetic Such a mind
    Vital, though metaphysical –

To Such, such an event, I think
    Would cause unscientific pain:
Science, appalled by thought, would shrink
    To its component parts again.

The Florist Rose

This wax-mannequin nude, the florist rose,
She of the long stem and too glossy leaf,
Is dead to honest greenfly and leaf-cutter:
Behind plate-glass watches the yellow fogs.

Claims kin with the robust male aeroplane
Whom eagles hate and phantoms of the air,
Who has no legend, as she breaks from legend –
From fellowship with sword and sail and crown.

Experiment's flower, scentless (he its bird);
Is dewed by the spray-gun; is tender-thorned;
Pouts, false-virginal, between bud and bloom;
Bought as a love-gift, droops within the day.

Lost Acres

These acres, always again lost
   By every new ordnance-survey
And searched for at exhausting cost
   Of time and thought, are still away.

They have their paper-substitute –
   Intercalation of an inch
At the so-many-thousandth foot:
   And no one parish feels the pinch.

But lost they are, despite all care,
   And perhaps likely to be bound
Together in a piece somewhere,
   A plot of undiscovered ground.

Invisible, they have the spite
   To swerve the tautest measuring-chain
And the exact theodolite
   Perched every side of them in vain.

Yet, be assured, we have no need
   To plot these acres of the mind
With prehistoric fern and reed
   And monsters such as heroes find.

Maybe they have their flowers, their birds,
   Their trees behind the phantom fence,
But of a substance without words:
   To walk there would be loss of sense.

At First Sight

'Love at first sight,' some say, misnaming
Discovery of twinned helplessness
Against the huge tug of procreation.

But friendship at first sight? This also
Catches fiercely at the surprised heart
So that the cheek blanches and then blushes.

Recalling War

Entrance and exit wounds are silvered clean,
The track aches only when the rain reminds.
The one-legged man forgets his leg of wood,
The one-armed man his jointed wooden arm.
The blinded man sees with his ears and hands
As much or more than once with both his eyes.
Their war was fought these twenty years ago
And now assumes the nature-look of time,
As when the morning traveller turns and views
His wild night-stumbling carved into a hill.

What, then, was war? No mere discord of flags
But an infection of the common sky
That sagged ominously upon the earth
Even when the season was the airiest May.
Down pressed the sky, and we, oppressed, thrust out
Boastful tongue, clenched fist and valiant yard.
Natural infirmities were out of mode,
For Death was young again: patron alone
Of healthy dying, premature fate-spasm.

Fear made fine bed-fellows. Sick with delight
At life's discovered transitoriness,
Our youth became all-flesh and waived the mind.
Never was such antiqueness of romance,
Such tasty honey oozing from the heart.
And old importances came swimming back –
Wine, meat, log-fires, a roof over the head,
A weapon at the thigh, surgeons at call.
Even there was a use again for God –
A word of rage in lack of meat, wine, fire,
In ache of wounds beyond all surgeoning.

War was return of earth to ugly earth,
War was foundering of sublimities,
Extinction of each happy art and faith
By which the world had still kept head in air,
Protesting logic or protesting love,
Until the unendurable moment struck –
The inward scream, the duty to run mad.

And we recall the merry ways of guns –
Nibbling the walls of factory and church
Like a child, piecrust; felling groves of trees
Like a child, dandelions with a switch.
Machine-guns rattle toy-like from a hill,
Down in a row the brave tin-soldiers fall:
A sight to be recalled in elder days
When learnedly the future we devote
To yet more boastful visions of despair.

Down, Wanton, Down!

Down, wanton, down! Have you no shame
That at the whisper of Love's name,
Or Beauty's, presto! up you raise
Your angry head and stand at gaze?

Poor bombard-captain, sworn to reach
The ravelin and effect a breach –
Indifferent what you storm or why,
So be that in the breach you die!

Love may be blind, but Love at least
Knows what is man and what mere beast;
Or Beauty wayward, but requires
More delicacy from her squires.

Tell me, my witless, whose one boast
Could be your staunchness at the post,
When were you made a man of parts
To think fine and profess the arts?

Will many-gifted Beauty come
Bowing to your bald rule of thumb,
Or Love swear loyalty to your crown?
Be gone, have done! Down, wanton, down!

And glad to find, on again looking at it,
It meant even less to me than I had thought –
You know the ship is moving when you see
The boxes on the quayside sliding away
And growing smaller – and feel a calm delight
When the port's cleared and the coast out of sight,
And ships are few, each on its proper course,
With no occasion for approach or discourse.

Nature's Lineaments

When mountain rocks and leafy trees
And clouds and things like these,
With edges,

Caricature the human face,
Such scribblings have no grace
Nor peace –

The bulbous nose, the sunken chin,
The ragged mouth in grin
Of cretin.

Nature is always so: you find
That all she has of mind
Is wind,

Retching among the empty spaces,
Ruffling the idiot grasses,
The sheep's fleeces.

Whose pleasures are excreting, poking,
Havocking and sucking,
Sleepy licking.

Whose griefs are melancholy,
Whose flowers are oafish,
Whose waters, silly,
Whose birds, raffish,
Whose fish, fish.

Time

The vague sea thuds against the marble cliffs
And from their fragments age-long grinds
Pebbles like flowers.

Or the vague weather wanders in the fields,
And up spring flowers with coloured buds
Like marble pebbles.

The beauty of the flowers is Time, death-grieved?
The pebbles' beauty too is Time,
Life-wearied.

It is easy to admire a blowing flower
Or a smooth pebble flower-like freaked
By Time and vagueness.

Time is Time's lapse, the emulsive element coaxing
All obstinate locks and rusty hinges
To loving-kindness.

And am I proof against that lovesome pair,
Old age and childhood, twins in Time,
In sorrowful vagueness?

And will I not pretend the accustomed thanks:
Humouring age with filial flowers,
Childhood with pebbles?

The Philosopher

Three blank walls, a barred window with no view,
A ceiling within reach of the raised hands,
A floor blank as the walls.

And, ruling out distraction of the body –
Growth of the hair and nails, a prison diet,
Thoughts of escape –

Ruling out memory and fantasy,
The distant tramping of the gaoler's boots,
Visiting mice and such,

What solace here for a laborious mind!
What a redoubtable and single task
One might attempt here:

Threading a logic between wall and wall,
Ceiling and floor, more accurate by far
Than the cob-spider's.

Truth captured without increment of flies –
Spinning and knotting till the cell became
A spacious other head

In which the emancipated reason might
Learn in due time to walk at greater length
And more unanswerably.

On Dwelling

Courtesies of good-morning and good-evening
From rustic lips fail as the town encroaches:
Soon nothing passes but the cold quick stare
Of eyes that see ghosts, yet too many for fear.

Here I too walk, silent myself, in wonder
At a town not mine, though plainly coextensive
With mine, even in days coincident:
In mine I dwell, in theirs like them I haunt.

And the green country, should I turn again there?
My bumpkin neighbours loom even ghostlier:
Like trees they murmur or like blackbirds sing
Courtesies of good-morning and good-evening.

Parent to Children

When you grow up, are no more children,
Nor am I then your parent:
The day of settlement falls.

'Parent', mortality's reminder,
In each son's mouth or daughter's
A word of shame and rage!

I, who begot you, ask no pardon of you;
Nor may the soldier ask
Pardon of the strewn dead.

The procreative act was blind:
It was not you I sired then –
For who sires friends, as you are mine now?

In fear begotten, I begot in fear.
Would you have had me cast fear out
So that you should not be?

Ogres and Pygmies

Those famous men of old, the Ogres –
They had long beards and stinking arm-pits,
They were wide-mouthed, long-yarded and great-bellied
Yet of no taller stature, Sirs, than you.
They lived on Ogre-Strand, which was no place
But the churl's terror of their vast extent,
Where every foot was three-and-thirty inches
And every penny bought a whole hog.
Now of their company none survive, not one,
The times being, thank God, unfavourable
To all but nightmare shadows of their fame;
Their images stand howling on the hill
(The winds enforced against those wide mouths),
Whose granite haunches country-folk salute
With May Day kisses, and whose knobbed knees.

So many feats they did to admiration:
With their enormous throats they sang louder
Than ten cathedral choirs, with their grand yards
Stormed the most rare and obstinate maidenheads,
With their strong-gutted and capacious bellies
Digested stones and glass like ostriches.
They dug great pits and heaped huge mounds,
Deflected rivers, wrestled with the bear
And hammered judgements for posterity –
For the sweet-cupid-lipped and tassel-yarded
Delicate-stomached dwellers
In Pygmy Alley, where with brooding on them
A foot is shrunk to seven inches
And twelve-pence will not buy a spare rib.
And who would judge between Ogres and Pygmies –
The thundering text, the snivelling commentary –
Reading between such covers he will marvel
How his own members bloat and shrink again.

To Walk on Hills

To walk on hills is to employ legs
As porters of the head and heart
Jointly adventuring towards
Perhaps true equanimity.

To walk on hills is to see sights
And hear sounds unfamiliar.
When in wind the pine-tree roars,
When crags with bleatings echo,
When water foams below the fall,
Heart records that journey
As memorable indeed;
Head reserves opinion,
Confused by the wind.

A view of three shires and the sea!
Seldom so much at once appears
Of the coloured world, says heart.
Head is glum, says nothing.

Legs become weary, halting
To sprawl in a rock's shelter,
While the sun drowsily blinks
On head at last brought low –
This giddied passenger of legs
That has no word to utter.

Heart does double duty,
As heart, and as head,
With portentous trifling.
A castle, on its crag perched,
Across the miles between is viewed
With awe as across years.

Now a daisy pleases,
Pleases and astounds, even,
That on a garden lawn could blow
All summer long with no esteem.

And the buzzard's cruel poise,
And the plover's misery,
And the important beetle's
Blue-green-shiny back. . . .

To walk on hills is to employ legs
To march away and lose the day.
Confess, have you known shepherds?
And are they not a witless race,
Prone to quaint visions?
Not thus from solitude
(Solitude sobers only)
But from long hilltop striding.

To Bring the Dead to Life

To bring the dead to life
Is no great magic.
Few are wholly dead:
Blow on a dead man's embers
And a live flame will start.

Let his forgotten griefs be now,
And now his withered hopes;
Subdue your pen to his handwriting
Until it prove as natural
To sign his name as yours.

Limp as he limped,
Swear by the oaths he swore;
If he wore black, affect the same;
If he had gouty fingers,
Be yours gouty too.

Assemble tokens intimate of him –
A seal, a cloak, a pen:
Around these elements then build
A home familiar to
The greedy revenant.

So grant him life, but reckon
That the grave which housed him
May not be empty now!
You in his spotted garments
Shall yourself lie wrapped.

To Evoke Posterity

To evoke posterity
Is to weep on your own grave,
Ventriloquizing for the unborn:
'Would you were present in flesh, hero!
What wreaths and junketings!'

And the punishment is fixed:
To be found fully ancestral,
To be cast in bronze for a city square,
To dribble green in times of rain
And stain the pedestal.

Spiders in the spread beard;
A life proverbial
On clergy lips a-cackle;
Eponymous institutes,
Their luckless architecture.

Two more dates of life and birth
For the hour of special study
From which all boys and girls of mettle
Twice a week play truant
And worn excuses try.

Alive, you have abhorred
The crowds on holiday
Jostling and whistling – yet would you air
Your death-mask, smoothly lidded,
Along the promenade?

Any Honest Housewife

Any honest housewife could sort them out,
Having a nose for fish, an eye for apples.
Is it any mystery who are the sound,
And who the rotten? Never, by her lights.

Any honest housewife who, by ill-fortune,
Ever engaged a slut to scrub for her
Could instantly distinguish from the workers
The lazy, the liars and the petty thieves.

Does this denote a sixth peculiar sense
Gifted to housewives for their vestal needs?
Or is it failure of the usual five
In all unthrifty writers on this head?

Defeat of the Rebels

The enemy forces are in wild flight.
Pour souls (you say), they were intoxicated
With rhetoric and banners, thought it enough
To believe and to blow trumpets, to wear
That menacing lie in their shakos.

Enough: it falls to us to shoot them down,
The incorrigibles and cowards,
Where they shiver behind rocks, or in ditches
Seek graves that have no headstones to them –
Such prisoners were unprofitable.

Now as our vanguard, pressing on,
Dislodges them from village and town,
Who yelling abandon packs and cloaks,
Their arms and even the day's rations,
We are not abashed by victory,

We raise no pitying monument
To check the counter-stroke of fortune.
These are not spoils: we recognize
Our own strewn gear, that never had been robbed
But for our sloth and hesitancy.

Twined together and, as is customary,
For words of rapture groping, they
'Never such love,' swore, 'ever before was!'
Contrast with all loves that had failed or staled
Registered their own as love indeed.

And was this not to blab idly
The heart's fated inconstancy?
Better in love to seal the love-sure lips,
For truly love was before words were,
And no word given, no word broken.

When the name 'love' is uttered
(Love, the near-honourable malady
With which in greed and haste they
Each other do infect and curse)
Or, worse, is written down. . . .

Wise after the event, by love withered,
A 'never more!' most frantically
Sorrow and shame would proclaim
Such as, they'd swear, never before were:
True lovers even in this.

The China Plate

From a crowded barrow in a street-market
The plate was ransomed for a few coppers,
Was brought gleefully home, given a place
On a commanding shelf.

'Quite a museum-piece,' an expert cries
(Eyeing it through the ready pocket-lens) –
As though a glass case would be less sepulchral
Than the barrow-hearse!

For weeks this plate retells the history
Whenever an eye runs in that direction:
'Near perdition I was, in a street-market
With rags and old shoes.'

'A few coppers' – here once again
The purchaser's proud hand lifts down
The bargain, displays the pot-bank sign
Scrawled raggedly underneath.

Enough, permit the treasure to forget
The emotion of that providential purchase,
Becoming a good citizen of the house
Like its fellow-crockery.

Let it dispense sandwiches at a party
And not be noticed in the drunken buzz,
Or little cakes at afternoon tea
When cakes are in demand.

Let it regain a lost habit of life,
Foreseeing death in honourable breakage
Somewhere between the kitchen and the shelf
To be sincerely mourned.

Certain Mercies

Now must all satisfaction
Appear mere mitigation
Of an accepted curse?

Must we henceforth be grateful
That the guards, though spiteful,
Are slow of foot and wit?

That by night we may spread
Over the plank bed
A thin coverlet?

That the rusty water
In the unclean pitcher
Our thirst quenches?

That the rotten, detestable
Food is yet eatable
By us ravenous?

That the prison censor
Permits a weekly letter?
(We may write: 'we are well.')

That, with patience and deference,
We do not experience
The punishment cell?

That each new indignity
Defeats only the body,
Pampering the spirit
With obscure, proud merit?

The Cuirassiers of the Frontier

Goths, Vandals, Huns, Isaurian mountaineers,
Made Roman by our Roman sacrament,
We can know little (as we care little)
Of the Metropolis: her candled churches,
Her white-gowned pederastic senators,
The cut-throat factions of her Hippodrome,
The eunuchs of her draped saloons.

Here is the frontier, here our camp and place –
Beans for the pot, fodder for horses,
And Roman arms. Enough. He who among us
At full gallop, the bowstring to his ear,
Lets drive his heavy arrows, to sink
Stinging through Persian corslets damascened,
Then follows with the lance – he has our love.

The Christ bade Holy Peter sheathe his sword,
Being outnumbered by the Temple guard.
And this was prudence, the cause not yet lost
While Peter might persuade the crowd to rescue.
Peter renegued, breaking his sacrament.
With us the penalty is death by stoning,
Not to be made a bishop.

In Peter's Church there is no faith nor truth,
Nor justice anywhere in palace or court.
That we continue watchful on the rampart
Concerns no priest.   A gaping silken dragon,
Puffed by the wind, suffices us for God.
We, not the City, are the Empire's soul:
A rotten tree lives only in its rind.

The Laureate

Like a lizard in the sun, though not scuttling
When men approach, this wretch, this thing of rage,
Scowls and sits rhyming in his horny age.

His time and truth he has not bridged to ours,
But shrivelled by long heliotropic idling
He croaks at us his out-of-date humours.

Once long ago here was a poet; who died.
See how remorse twitching his mouth proclaims
It was no natural death, but suicide.

Arrogant, lean, unvenerable, he
Still turns for comfort to the western flames
That glitter a cold span above the sea.

A Jealous Man

To be homeless is a pride
To the jealous man prowling
Hungry down the night lanes,

Who has no steel at his side,
No drink hot in his mouth,
But a mind dream-enlarged,

Who witnesses warfare,
Man with woman, hugely
Raging from hedge to hedge:

The raw knotted oak-club
Clenched in the raw fist,
The ivy-noose well flung,

The thronged din of battle,
Gaspings of the throat-snared,
Snores of the battered dying,

Tall corpses, braced together,
Fallen in clammy furrows,
Male and female,

Or, among haulms of nettle
Humped, in noisome heaps,
Male and female.

He glowers in the choked roadway
Between twin churchyards,
Like a turnip ghost.

(Here, the rain-worn headstone,
There, the Celtic cross
In rank white marble.)

This jealous man is smitten,
His fear-jerked forehead
Sweats a fine musk;

A score of bats bewitched
By the ruttish odour
Swoop singing at his head;

Nuns bricked up alive
Within the neighbouring wall
Wail in cat-like longing.

Crows, cocks, crow loud!
Reprieve the doomed devil,
Has he not died enough?

Now, out of careless sleep,
She wakes and greets him coldly,
The woman at home,

She, with a private wonder
At shoes bemired and bloody –
His war was not hers.

The Cloak

Into exile with only a few shirts,
Some gold coin and the necessary papers.
But winds are contrary: the Channel packet
Time after time returns the sea-sick peer
To Sandwich, Deal or Rye. He does not land,
But keeps his cabin: so at last we find him
In humble lodgings at perhaps Dieppe,
His shirts unpacked, his night-cap on a peg,
Passing the day with cards and swordsmanship
Or merry passages with chambermaids,
By night at his old work. And all is well –
The country wine wholesome although so sharp,
And French his second tongue; a faithful valet
Brushes his hat and brings him newspapers.
This nobleman is at home anywhere,
His castle being, the valet says, his title.
The cares of an estate would incommode
Such tasks as now his Lordship has in hand.
His Lordship, says the valet, contemplates
A profitable absence of some years.
Has he no friend at Court to intercede?
He wants none: exile's but another name
For an old habit of non-residence
In all but the recesses of his cloak.
It was this angered a great personage.

The Foreboding

Looking by chance in at the open window
    I saw my own self seated in his chair
With gaze abstracted, furrowed forehead,
    Unkempt hair.

I thought that I had suddenly come to die,
    That to a cold corpse this was my farewell,
Until the pen moved slowly upon paper
    And tears fell.

He had written a name, yours, in printed letters:
    One word on which bemusedly to pore –
No protest, no desire, your naked name,
    Nothing more.

Would it be tomorrow, would it be next year?
    But the vision was not false, this much I knew;
And I turned angrily from the open window
    Aghast at you.

Why never a warning, either by speech or look,
    That the love you cruelly gave me could not last?
Already it was too late: the bait swallowed,
    The hook fast.

With Her Lips Only

This honest wife, challenged at dusk
At the garden gate, under a moon perhaps,
In scent of honeysuckle, dared to deny
Love to an urgent lover: with her lips only,
Not with her heart. It was no assignation;
Taken aback, what could she say else?
For the children's sake, the lie was venial;
'For the children's sake', she argued with her conscience.

Yet a mortal lie must follow before dawn:
Challenged as usual in her own bed,
She protests love to an urgent husband,
Not with her heart but with her lips only;
'For the children's sake', she argues with her conscience,
'For the children' – turning suddenly cold towards them.

The Halls of Bedlam

Forewarned of madness:
In three days' time at dusk
The fit masters him.

How to endure those days?
(Forewarned is foremad)
'– Normally, normally.'

He will gossip with children,
Argue with elders,
Check the cash account.

'I shall go mad that day –'
The gossip, the argument,
The neat marginal entry.

His case is not uncommon,
The doctors pronounce;
But prescribe no cure.

To be mad is not easy,
Will earn him no money,
But a niche in the news.

Then to-morrow, children,
To-morrow or the next day
He resigns from the firm.

His boyhood's ambition
Was to become an artist –
Like any City man's.

To the walls and halls of Bedlam
The artist is welcome –
Bold brush and full palette.

Through the cell's grating
He will watch his children
To and from school.

'Suffer the little children
To come unto me
With their Florentine hair!'

A very special story
For their very special friends –
They burst in the telling:

Of an evil thing, armed,
Tap-tapping on the door,
Tap-tapping on the floor,
'On the third day at dusk.'

Father in his shirt-sleeves
Flourishing a hatchet –
Run, children, run!

No one could stop him,
No one understood;
And in the evening papers. . . .

(Imminent genius,
Troubles at the office,
Normally, normally,
As if already mad.)

A Country Mansion

This ancient house so notable
For its gables and great staircase,
Its mulberry-trees and alleys of clipped yew,
Humbles the show of every near demesne.

At the beginning it acknowledged owners –
Father, son, grandson –
But then, surviving the last heirs of the line,
Became a place for life-tenancy only.

At the beginning, no hint of fate,
No rats and no hauntings;
In the garden, then, the fruit-trees grew
Slender and similar in long rows.

A bedroom with a low ceiling
Caused little fret at first;
But gradual generations of discomfort
Have bred an anger there to stifle sleep.

And the venerable dining-room,
Where port in Limerick glasses
Glows twice as red reflected
In the memory-mirror of the waxed table –

For a time with paint and flowered paper
A mistress tamed its walls,
But pious antiquarian hands, groping,
Rediscovered the grey panels beneath.

Children love the old house tearfully,
And the parterres, how fertile!
Married couples under the testers hugging
Enjoy carnality's bliss as nowhere else.

A smell of mould from loft to cellar,
Yet sap still brisk in the oak
Of the great beams: if ever they use a saw
It will stain, as cutting a branch from a green tree.

. . . Old Parr had lived one hundred years and five
(So to King Charles he bragged)
When he did open penance, in a sheet,
For fornication with posterity.

Old Parr died; not so this mansion
Whose inhabitants, bewitched,
Pour their fresh blood through its historic veins
And, if a tile blow from the roof, tremble.

The last-born of this race of sacristans
Broke the long spell, departed;
They lay his knife and fork at every meal
And every evening warm his bed;

Yet cannot draw him back from the far roads
For trifling by the lily-pool
Or wine at the hushed table where they meet,
The guests of genealogy.

It was his childhood's pleasure-ground
And still may claim his corpse,
Yet foster-cradle or foster-grave
He will not count as home.

This rebel does not hate the house,
Nor its dusty joys impugn:
No place less reverend could provoke
So proud an absence from it.

He has that new malaise of time:
Gratitude choking with vexation
That he should opulently inherit
The goods and titles of the extinct.

Lovers in Winter

The posture of the tree
    Shows the prevailing wind;
And ours, long misery
    When you are long unkind.

But forward, look, we lean –
    Not backward as in doubt –
And still with branches green
    Ride our ill weather out.

Advocates

Fugitive firs and larches for a moment
Caught, past midnight, by our headlight beam
On that mad journey through unlasting lands
I cannot put a name to, years ago,
(And my companions drowsy-drunk) – these trees
Resume again their sharp appearance, perfect
Of spur and tassel, claiming memory,
Claiming affection: 'Will we be included
In the catalogue? Yes, yes?' they plead.
Green things, you are already there enrolled.
And should a new resentment gnaw in me
Against my dear companions of that journey
(Strangers already then, in thought and deed)
You shall be advocates, charged to deny
That all the good I lived with them is lost.

On Portents

If strange things happen where she is,
So that men say that graves open,
And the dead walk, or that futurity
Becomes a womb and the unborn are shed,
Such portents are not to be wondered at,
Being tourbillions in Time made
By the strong pulling of her bladed mind
Through that ever-reluctant element.

The Terraced Valley

In a deep thought of you and concentration
I came by hazard to a new region:
The unnecessary sun was not there,
The necessary earth lay without care –
For more than sunshine warmed the skin
Of the round world that was turned outside-in.

Calm sea beyond the terraced valley
Without horizon easily was spread,
As it were overhead,
Washing the mountain-spurs behind me:
The unnecessary sky was not there,
Therefore no heights, no deeps, no birds of the air.

Neat outside-inside, neat below-above,
Hermaphrodizing love.
Neat this-way-that-way and without mistake:
On the right hand could slide the left glove.
Neat over-under: the young snake
Through an unyielding shell his path could break.
Singing of kettles, like a singing brook,
Made out-of-doors a fireside nook.

But you, my love, where had you then your station?
Seeing that on this counter-earth together
We go not distant from each other;
I knew you near me in that strange region,
So searched for you, in hope to see you stand
On some near olive-terrace, in the heat,
The left-hand glove drawn on your right hand,
The empty snake's egg perfect at your feet –

But found you nowhere in the wide land,

And cried disconsolately, until you spoke
Immediate at my elbow, and your voice broke
This trick of time, changing the world about
To once more inside-in and outside-out.

The Chink

A sunbeam on the well-waxed oak,
    In shape resembling not at all
The ragged chink by which it broke
    Into this darkened hall,
Swims round and golden over me,
    The sun's plenipotentiary.

So may my round love a chink find :
    With such address to break
Into your grief-occluded mind
    As you shall not mistake
But, rising, open to me for truth's sake.

The Ages of Oath

To find a garden-tulip growing
Among wild primroses of a wild field,
Or a cuckoo's egg in a blackbird's nest,
Or a giant mushroom, a whole basketful –
The memorable feats of childhood!
Once, by the earthworks, scratching in the soil,
My stick turned up a Roman amber bead. . . .

The lost, the freakish, the unspelt
Drew me: for simple sights I had no eye.
And did I swear allegiance then
To wildness, not (as I thought) to truth –
Become a virtuoso, and this also,
Later, of simple sights, when tiring
Of unicorn and upas?

Did I forget how to greet plainly
The especial sight, how to know deeply
The pleasure shared by upright hearts?
And is this to begin afresh, with oaths
On the true book, in the true name,
Now stammering out my praise of you,
Like a boy owning his first love?

She, then, like snow in a dark night,
Fell secretly. And the world waked
With dazzling of the drowsy eye,
So that some muttered 'Too much light,'
And drew the curtains close.
Like snow, warmer than fingers feared,
And to soil friendly;
Holding the histories of the night
In yet unmelted tracks.

End of Play

We have reached the end of pastime, for always,
Ourselves and everyone, though few confess it
Or see the sky other than, as of old,
A foolish smiling Mary-mantle blue;

Though life may still seem to dawdle golden
In some June landscape among giant flowers,
The grass to shine as cruelly green as ever,
Faith to descend in a chariot from the sky –

May seem only: a mirror and an echo
Mediate henceforth with vision and sound.
The cry of faith, no longer mettlesome,
Sounds as a blind man's pitiful plea of 'blind'.

We have at last ceased idling, which to regret
Were as shallow as to ask our milk-teeth back;
As many forthwith do, and on their knees
Call lugubriously upon chaste Christ.

We tell no lies now, at last cannot be
The rogues we were – so evilly linked in sense
With what we scrutinized that lion or tiger
Could leap from every copse, strike and devour us.

No more shall love in hypocritic pomp
Conduct its innocents through a dance of shame,
From timid touching of gloved fingers
To frantic laceration of naked breasts.

Yet love survives, the word carved on a sill
Under antique dread of the headsman's axe;
It is the echoing mind, as in the mirror
We stare on our dazed trunks at the block kneeling.

The Fallen Tower of Siloam

Should the building totter, run for an archway!
We were there already – already the collapse
Powdered the air with chalk, and shrieking
Of old men crushed under the fallen beams
Dwindled to comic yelps. How unterrible
When the event outran the alarm
And suddenly we were free –

Free to forget how grim it stood,
That tower, and what wide fissures ran
Up the west wall, how rotten the under-pinning
At the south-eastern angle. Satire
Had whirled a gentle wind around it,
As if to buttress the worn masonry;
Yet we, waiting, had abstained from satire.

It behoved us, indeed, as poets
To be silent in Siloam, to foretell
No visible calamity. Though kings
Were crowned and gold coin minted still and horses
Still munched at nose-bags in the public streets,
All such sad emblems were to be condoned:
An old wives' tale, not ours.

The Great-Grandmother

That aged woman with the bass voice
And yellowing white hair: believe her.
Though to your grandfather, her son, she lied
And to your father disingenuously
Told half the tale as the whole,
Yet she was honest with herself,
Knew disclosure was not yet due,
Knows it is due now.

She will conceal nothing of consequence
From you, her great-grandchildren
(So distant the relationship,
So near her term),
Will tell you frankly, she has waited
Only for your sincere indifference
To exorcize that filial regard
Which has estranged her, seventy years,
From the folk of her house.

Confessions of old distaste
For music, sighs and roses –
Their false-innocence assaulting her,
Breaching her hard heart;
Of the pleasures of a full purse,
Of clean brass and clean linen,
Of being alone at last;
Disgust with the ailing poor
To whom she was bountiful;
How the prattle of young children
Vexed more than if they whined;
How she preferred cats.

She will say, yes, she acted well,
Took such pride in the art

That none of them suspected, even,
Her wrathful irony
In doing what they asked
Better than they could ask it . . .
But, ah, how grudgingly her will returned
After the severance of each navel-cord,
And fled how far again,
When again she was kind!

She has outlasted all man-uses,
As was her first resolve:
Happy and idle like a port
After the sea's recession,
She does not misconceive the nature
Of shipmen or of ships.
Hear her, therefore, as the latest voice;
The intervening generations (drifting
On tides of fancy still), ignore.

No More Ghosts

The patriarchal bed with four posts
Which was a harbourage of ghosts
Is hauled out from the attic glooms
And cut to wholesome furniture for wholesome rooms;

Where they (the ghosts) confused, abused, thinned,
Forgetful how they sighed and sinned,
Cannot disturb our ordered ease
Except as summer dust tickles the nose to sneeze.

We are restored to simple days, are free
From cramps of dark necessity,
And one another recognize
By an immediate love that signals at our eyes.

No new ghosts can appear. Their poor cause
Was that time freezes, and time thaws;
But here only such loves can last
As do not ride upon the weathers of the past.

A Love Story

The full moon easterly rising, furious,
Against a winter sky ragged with red;
The hedges high in snow, and owls raving –
Solemnities not easy to withstand:
A shiver wakes the spine.

In boyhood, having encountered the scene,
I suffered horror: I fetched the moon home,
With owls and snow, to nurse in my head
Throughout the trials of a new spring,
Famine unassuaged.

But fell in love, and made a lodgement
Of love on those chill ramparts.
Her image was my ensign: snows melted,
Hedges sprouted, the moon tenderly shone,
The owls trilled with tongues of nightingale.

These were all lies, though they matched the time,
And brought me less than luck: her image
Warped in the weather, turned beldamish.
Then back came winter on me at a bound,
The pallid sky heaved with a moon-quake.

Dangerous it has been with love-notes
To serenade Queen Famine.
In tears I recomposed the former scene,
Let the snow lie, watched the moon rise, suffered
    the owls,
Paid homage to them of unevent.

Dawn Bombardment

Guns from the sea open against us:
The smoke rocks bodily in the casemate
And a yell of doom goes up.
We count and bless each new, heavy concussion –
Captives awaiting rescue.

Visiting angel of the wild-fire hair
Who in dream reassured us nightly
Where we lay fettered,
Laugh at us, as we wake – our faces
So tense with hope the tears run down.

The Shot

The curious heart plays with its fears:
To hurl a shot through the ship's planks,
Being assured that the green angry flood
Is charmed and dares not dance into the hold –
Nor first to sweep a lingering glance around
For land or shoal or cask adrift.
'So miracles are done; but madmen drown.'

O weary luxury of hypothesis –
For human nature, honest human nature
(Which the fear-pampered heart denies)
Knows its own miracle: not to go mad.
Will pitch the shot in fancy, hint the fact,
Will bore perhaps a meagre auger hole
But stanch the spurting with a tarred rag,
And will not drown, nor even ride the cask.

The Thieves

Lovers in the act dispense
With such meum-teum sense
As might warningly reveal
What they must not pick or steal,
And their nostrum is to say:
'I and you are both away.'

After, when they disentwine
You from me and yours from mine,
Neither can be certain who
Was that I whose mine was you.
To the act again they go
More completely not to know.

Theft is theft and raid is raid
Though reciprocally made.
Lovers, the conclusion is
Doubled sighs and jealousies
In a single heart that grieves
For lost honour among thieves.

Lollocks

By sloth on sorrow fathered,
These dusty-featured Lollocks
Have their nativity in all disordered
Backs of cupboard drawers.

They play hide and seek
Among collars and novels
And empty medicine bottles,
And letters from abroad
That never will be answered.

Every sultry night
They plague little children,
Gurgling from the cistern,
Humming from the air,
Skewing up the bed-clothes,
Twitching the blind.

When the imbecile agèd
Are over-long in dying
And the nurse drowses,
Lollocks come skipping
Up the tattered stairs
And are nasty together
In the bed's shadow.

The signs of their presence
Are boils on the neck,
Dreams of vexation suddenly recalled
In the middle of the morning,
Languor after food.

Men cannot see them,
Men cannot hear them,
Do not believe in them –

But suffer the more,
Both in neck and belly.

Women can see them –
O those naughty wives
Who sit by the fireside
Munching bread and honey,
Watching them in mischief
From corners of their eyes,
Slily allowing them to lick
Honey-sticky fingers.

Sovereign against Lollocks
Are hard broom and soft broom,
To well comb the hair,
To well brush the shoe,
And to pay every debt
As it falls due.

To Sleep

The mind's eye sees as the heart mirrors:
Loving in part, I did not see you whole,
Grew flesh-enraged that I could not conjure
A whole you to attend my fever-fit
In the doubtful hour between a night and day
And be Sleep that had kept so long away.

Of you sometimes a hand, a brooch, a shoe
Wavered beside me, unarticulated –
As the vexed insomniac dream-forges;
And the words I chose for your voice to speak
Echoed my own voice with its dry creak.

Now that I love you, now that I recall
All scattered elements of will that swooped
By night as jealous dreams through windows
To circle above the beds like bats,
Or as dawn-birds flew blindly at the panes
In curiosity rattling out their brains –

Now that I love you, as not before,
Now you can be and say, as not before:
The mind clears and the heart true-mirrors you
Where at my side an early watch you keep
And all self-bruising heads loll into sleep.

Despite and Still

Have you not read
The words in my head,
And I made part
Of your own heart?
We have been such as draw
The losing straw –
You of your gentleness,
I of my rashness,
Both of despair –
Yet still might share
This happy will:
To love despite and still.
Never let us deny
The thing's necessity,
But, O, refuse
To choose
Where chance may seem to give
Loves in alternative.

The Suicide in the Copse

The suicide, far from content,
Stared down at his own shattered skull:
Was this what he meant?

Had not his purpose been
To liberate himself from duns and dolts
By a change of scene?

From somewhere came a roll of laughter:
He had looked so on his wedding-day,
And the day after.

There was nowhere at all to go,
And no diversion now but to peruse
What literature the winds might blow

Into the copse where his body lay:
A year-old sheet of sporting news,
A crumped schoolboy essay.

Frightened Men

We were not ever of their feline race,
Never had hidden claws so sharp as theirs
In any half-remembered incarnation;
Have only the least knowledge of their minds
Through a grace on their part in thinking aloud;
And we remain mouse-quiet when they begin
Suddenly in their unpredictable way
To weave an allegory of their lives,
Making each point by walking round it –
Then off again, as interest is warmed.
What have they said? Or unsaid? What?
We understood the general drift only.

They are punctilious as implacable,
Most neighbourly to those who love them least.
A shout will scare them. When they spring, they seize.
The worst is when they hide from us and change
To something altogether other:
We meet them at the door, as who returns
After a one-hour-seeming century
To a house not his own.

Living among orchards, we are ruled
By the four seasons necessarily:
This from unseasonable frosts we learn
Or from usurping suns and haggard flowers –
Legitimist our disapproval.

Weather we knew, not seasons, in the city
Where, seasonless, orange and orchid shone,
Knew it by heavy overcoat or light,
Framed love in later terminologies
Than here, where we report how weight of snow,
Or weight of fruit, tears branches from the tree.

Mid-Winter Waking

Stirring suddenly from long hibernation,
I knew myself once more a poet
Guarded by timeless principalities
Against the worm of death, this hillside haunting;
And presently dared open both my eyes.

O gracious, lofty, shone against from under,
Back-of-the-mind-far clouds like towers;
And you, sudden warm airs that blow
Before the expected season of new blossom,
While sheep still gnaw at roots and lambless go –

Be witness that on waking, this mid-winter,
I found her hand in mine laid closely
Who shall watch out the Spring with me.
We stared in silence all around us
But found no winter anywhere to see.

The Beach

Louder than gulls the little children scream
Whom fathers haul into the jovial foam;
But others fearlessly rush in, breast high,
Laughing the salty water from their mouths –
Heroes of the nursery.

The horny boatman, who has seen whales
And flying fishes, who has sailed as far
As Demerara and the Ivory Coast,
Will warn them, when they crowd to hear his tales,
That every ocean smells alike of tar.

The Villagers and Death

The Rector's pallid neighbour at The Firs,
Death, did not flurry the parishioners.
Yet from a weight of superstitious fears
Each tried to lengthen his own term of years.
He was congratulated who combined
Toughness of flesh and weakness of the mind
In consequential rosiness of face.
This dull and not ill-mannered populace
Pulled off their caps to Death, as they slouched by,
But rumoured him both atheist and spy.
All vowed to outlast him (though none ever did)
And hear the earth drum on his coffin-lid.
Their groans and whispers down the village street
Soon soured his nature, which was never sweet.

The Door

When she came suddenly in
It seemed the door could never close again,
Nor even did she close it – she, she –
The room lay open to a visiting sea
Which no door could restrain.

Yet when at last she smiled, tilting her head
To take her leave of me,
Where she had smiled, instead
There was a dark door closing endlessly,
The waves receded.

Under the Pot

Sulkily the sticks burn, and though they crackle
   With scorn under the bubbling pot, or spout
Magnanimous jets of flame against the smoke,
   At each heel end a dirty sap breaks out.

Confess, creatures, how sulkily ourselves
   We hiss with doom, fuel of a sodden age –
Not rapt up roaring to the chimney stack
   On incandescent clouds of spirit or rage.

Through Nightmare

Never be disenchanted of
That place you sometimes dream yourself into,
Lying at large remove beyond all dream,
Or those you find there, though but seldom
In their company seated –

The untameable, the live, the gentle.
Have you not known them? Whom? They carry
Time looped so river-wise about their house
There's no way in by history's road
To name or number them.

In your sleepy eyes I read the journey
Of which disjointedly you tell; which stirs
My loving admiration, that you should travel
Through nightmare to a lost and moated land,
Who are timorous by nature.

She Tells Her Love While Half Asleep

She tells her love while half asleep,
  In the dark hours,
      With half-words whispered low:
As Earth stirs in her winter sleep
  And puts out grass and flowers
      Despite the snow,
      Despite the falling snow.

High on his figured couch beyond the waves
He dreams, in dream recalling her set walk
Down paths of oyster-shell bordered with flowers
And down the shadowy turf under the vine.
He sighs: 'Deep sunk in my erroneous past
She haunts the ruins and the ravaged lawns.'

Yet still unharmed it stands, the regal house
Crooked with age and overtopped by pines
Where first he wearied of her constancy.
And with a surer foot she goes than when
Dread of his hate was thunder in the air,
When the pines agonized with flaws of wind
And flowers glared up at her with frantic eyes.
Of him, now all is done, she never dreams
But calls a living blessing down upon
What he supposes rubble and rank grass;
Playing the queen to nobler company.

The Death Room

Look forward, truant, to your second childhood.
The crystal sphere discloses
Wall-paper roses mazily repeated
In pink and bronze, their bunches harbouring
Elusive faces, under an inconclusive
Circling, spidery, ceiling craquelure,
And, by the window-frame, the well-loathed, lame,
Damp-patch, cross-patch, sleepless L-for-Lemur
Who, puffed to giant size,
Waits jealously till children close their eyes.

To Juan at the Winter Solstice

There is one story and one story only
That will prove worth your telling,
Whether as learned bard or gifted child;
To it all lines or lesser gauds belong
That startle with their shining
Such common stories as they stray into.

Is it of trees you tell, their months and virtues,
Or strange beasts that beset you,
Of birds that croak at you the Triple will?
Or of the Zodiac and how slow it turns
Below the Boreal Crown,
Prison of all true kings that ever reigned?

Water to water, ark again to ark,
From woman back to woman:
So each new victim treads unfalteringly
The never altered circuit of his fate,
Bringing twelve peers as witness
Both to his starry rise and starry fall.

Or is it of the Virgin's silver beauty,
All fish below the thighs?
She in her left hand bears a leafy quince;
When, with her right she crooks a finger smiling,
How may the King hold back?
Royally then he barters life for love.

Or of the undying snake from chaos hatched,
Whose coils contain the ocean,
Into whose chops with naked sword he springs,
Then in black water, tangled by the reeds,
Battles three days and nights,
To be spewed up beside her scalloped shore?

Much snow is falling, winds roar hollowly,
The owl hoots from the elder,
Fear in your heart cries to the loving-cup:
Sorrow to sorrow as the sparks fly upward.
The log groans and confesses
There is one story and one story only.

Dwell on her graciousness, dwell on her smiling,
Do not forget what flowers
The great boar trampled down in ivy time.
Her brow was creamy as the crested wave,
Her sea-blue eyes were wild
But nothing promised that is not performed.

To be Called a Bear

Bears gash the forest trees
    To mark the bounds
    Of their own hunting grounds;
They follow the wild bees
    Point by point home
For love of honeycomb;
They browse on blueberries.

Then should I stare
If I am called a bear,
And it is not the truth?
Unkempt and surly with a sweet tooth
I tilt my muzzle toward the starry hub
Where Queen Callisto guards her cub,

But envy those that here
    All winter breathing slow
    Sleep warm under the snow,
That yawn awake when the skies clear,
    And lank with longing grow
No more than one brief month a year.

My Name and I

The impartial Law enrolled a name
    For my especial use:
My rights in it would rest the same
Whether I puffed it into fame
    Or sank it in abuse.

Robert was what my parents guessed
    When first they peered at me,
And *Graves* an honourable bequest
With Georgian silver and the rest
    From my male ancestry.

They taught me: 'You are *Robert Graves*
    (Which you must learn to spell),
But see that *Robert Graves* behaves,
Whether with honest men or knaves,
    Exemplarily well.'

Then though my I was always I,
    Illegal and unknown,
With nothing to arrest it by –
As will be obvious when I die
    And *Robert Graves* lives on –

I cannot well repudiate
    This noun, this natal star,
This gentlemanly self, this mate
So kindly forced on me by fate,
    Time and the registrar;

And therefore hurry him ahead
    As an ambassador
To fetch me home my beer and bread
Or commandeer the best green bed,
    As he has done before.

Yet, understand, I am not he
    Either in mind or limb;
My name will take less thought for me,
In worlds of men I cannot see,
    Than ever I for him.

At Viscount Nelson's lavish funeral,
　While the mob milled and yelled about St Paul's,
A General chatted with an Admiral:

'One of your Colleagues, Sir, remarked today
　That Nelson's *exit*, though to be lamented,
Falls not inopportunely, in its way.'

'He was a thorn in our flesh,' came the reply –
　'The most bird-witted, unaccountable,
Odd little runt that ever I did spy.

'One arm, one peeper, vain as Pretty Poll,
　A meddler, too, in foreign politics
And gave his heart in pawn to a plain moll.

'He would dare lecture us Sea Lords, and then
　Would treat his ratings as though men of honour
And play at leap-frog with his midshipmen!

'We tried to box him down, but up he popped,
　And when he'd banged Napoleon at the Nile
Became too much the hero to be dropped.

'You've heard that Copenhagen "blind eye" story?
　We'd tied him to Nurse Parker's apron-strings –
By G—d, he snipped them through and snatched the glory!'

'Yet,' cried the General, 'six-and-twenty sail
　Captured or sunk by him off Tráfalgár –
That writes a handsome *finis* to the tale.'

'Handsome enough. The seas are England's now.
　That fellow's foibles need no longer plague us.
He died most creditably, I'll allow.'

'And, Sir, the secret of his victories?'
　'By his unServicelike, familiar ways, Sir,
He made the whole Fleet love him, damn his eyes!'

The Persian Version

Truth-loving Persians do not dwell upon
The trivial skirmish fought near Marathon.
As for the Greek theatrical tradition
Which represents that summer's expedition
Not as a mere reconnaissance in force
By three brigades of foot and one of horse
(Their left flank covered by some obsolete
Light craft detached from the main Persian fleet)
But as a grandiose, ill-starred attempt
To conquer Greece – they treat it with contempt;
And only incidentally refute
Major Greek claims, by stressing what repute
The Persian monarch and the Persian nation
Won by this salutary demonstration:
Despite a strong defence and adverse weather
All arms combined magnificently together.

The Weather of Olympus

Zeus was once overheard to shout at Hera:
    'You hate it, do you? Well, I hate it worse –
East wind in May, sirocco all the Summer.
    Hell take this whole impossible Universe!'

A scholiast explains this warm rejoinder,
    Which sounds too man-like for Olympic use,
By noting that the snake-tailed chthonian winds
    Were answerable to Fate alone, not Zeus.

Grotesques

I

My Chinese uncle, gouty, deaf, half-blinded,
And more than a trifle absent-minded,
Astonished all St James's Square one day
By giving long and unexceptionably exact directions
To a little coolie girl, who'd lost her way.

II

The Lion-faced Boy at the Fair
And the Heir Apparent
Were equally slow at remembering people's faces.
But whenever they met, incognito, in the Brazilian
Pavilion, the Row and such-like places,
They exchanged, it is said, their sternest nods –
Like gods of dissimilar races.

III

Dr Newman with the crooked pince-nez
Had studied in Vienna and Chicago.
Chess was his only relaxation.
And Dr Newman remained unperturbed
By every nastier manifestation
Of plutodemocratic civilization:
All that was cranky, corny, ill-behaved,
Unnecessary, askew or orgiastic
Would creep unbidden to his side-door (hidden
Behind a poster in the Tube Station,
Nearly half-way up the moving-stairs),
Push its way in, to squat there undisturbed
Among box-files and tubular steel-chairs.
He was once seen at the Philharmonic Hall
Noting the reactions of two patients,

With pronounced paranoiac tendencies,
To old Dutch music. He appeared to recall
A tin of lozenges in his breast-pocket,
Put his hand confidently in –
And drew out a black imp, or sooterkin,
Six inches long, with one ear upside-down,
Licking at a vanilla ice-cream cornet –
Then put it back again with a slight frown.

IV

A Royal Duke, with no campaigning medals
To dignify his Orders, he would speak
Nostalgically at times of Mozambique
Where once the ship he cruised in ran aground:
How he drank cocoa, from a sailor's mug,
Poured from the common jug,
While loyal toasts went round.

V

Sir John addressed the Snake God in his temple,
Which was full of bats, not as a votary
But with the somewhat cynical courtesy,
Just short of condescension,
He might have paid the Governor-General
Of a small, hot, backward colony.
He was well versed in primitive religion,
But found this an embarrassing occasion:
The God was immense, noisy and affable,
Began to tickle him with a nervous chuckle,
Unfobbed a great gold clock for him to listen,
Hissed like a snake, and swallowed him at one mouthful.

VI

All horses on the racecourse of Tralee
    Have four more legs in gallop than in trot –

Two pairs fully extended, two pairs not;
And yet no thoroughbred with either three
    Or five legs but is mercilessly shot.
I watched a filly gnaw her fifth leg free,
Warned by a speaking mare since turned silentiary.

Conversation Piece

By moonlight
At midnight,
Under the vines,
A hotel chair
Settles down moodily before the headlines
Of a still-folded evening newspaper.

The other chair
Of the pair
Lies on its back,
Stiff as in pain,
Having been overturned with an angry crack;
And there till morning, alas, it must remain.

On the terrace
No blood-trace,
No sorry glitter
Of a knife, nothing:
Not even the fine-torn fragments of a letter
Or the dull gleam of a flung-off wedding-ring.

Still stable
On the table
Two long-stemmed glasses,
One full of drink,
Watch how the rat among the vines passes
And how the moon trembles on the crag's brink.

I'm through with You for Ever

The oddest, surely, of odd tales
    Recorded by the French
Concerns a sneak thief of Marseilles
    Tried by a callous Bench.

His youth, his innocency, his tears –
    No, nothing could abate
Their sentence of 'One hundred years
    In galleys of the State.'

Nevertheless, old wives affirm
    And annalists agree,
He sweated out the whole damned term,
    Bowed stiffly, and went free.

Then come, my angry love, review
    Your sentence of today.
'For ever' was unjust to you,
    The end too far away.

Give me four hundred years, or five –
    Can rage be so intense? –
And I will sweat them out alive
    To prove my impenitence.

Beauty in trouble flees to the good angel
   On whom she can rely
To pay her cab-fare, run a steaming bath,
   Poultice her bruised eye;

Will not at first, whether for shame or caution,
   Her difficulty disclose;
Until he draws a cheque book from his plumage,
   Asking her how much she owes;

(Breakfast in bed: coffee and marmalade,
   Toast, eggs, orange-juice,
After a long, sound sleep – the first since when? –
   And no word of abuse.)

Loves him less only than her saint-like mother,
   Promises to repay
His loans and most seraphic thoughtfulness
   A million-fold one day.

Beauty grows plump, renews her broken courage
   And, borrowing ink and pen,
Writes a news-letter to the evil angel
   (Her first gay act since when?):

The fiend who beats, betrays and sponges on her,
   Persuades her white is black,
Flaunts vespertilian wing and cloven hoof;
   And soon will fetch her back.

Virtue, good angel, is its own reward:
   Your dollars were well spent.
But would you to the marriage of true minds
   Admit impediment?

Sirocco at Deyá

How most unnatural-seeming, yet how proper:
The sea like a cat with fur rubbed the wrong way,
As the sirocco with its furnace flavour
Dashes at full tilt around the village
['From every-which-a-way, hot as a two-buck pistol']
Stripping green olives from the blown-back boughs,
Scorching the roses, blinding the eyes with sand;
While slanderous tongues in the small cafés
And in the tightly-shuttered granite houses
Clack defamation, incite and invite
Knives to consummate their near-murders . . .
Look up, a great grey cloud broods nonchalant
On the mountain-top nine hundred feet above us,
Motionless and turgid, blotting out the sun,
And from it sneers a supercilious Devil:
'Mere local wind: no messenger of mine!'

From the Embassy

I, an ambassador of Otherwhere
To the unfederated states of Here and There
Enjoy (as the phrase is)
Extra-territorial privileges.
With heres and theres I seldom come to blows
Or need, as once, to sandbag all my windows.
And though the Otherwhereish currency
Cannot be quoted yet officially,
I meet less hindrance now with the exchange
Nor is my garb, even, considered strange;
And shy enquiries for literature
Come in by every post, and the side door.

All saints revile her, and all sober men
Ruled by the God Apollo's golden mean –
In scorn of which we sailed to find her
In distant regions likeliest to hold her
Whom we desired above all things to know,
Sister of the mirage and echo.

It was a virtue not to stay,
To go our headstrong and heroic way
Seeking her out at the volcano's head,
Among pack ice, or where the track had faded
Beyond the cavern of the seven sleepers:
Whose broad high brow was white as any leper's,
Whose eyes were blue, with rowan-berry lips,
With hair curled honey-coloured to white hips.

The sap of Spring in the young wood a-stir
Will celebrate with green the Mother,
And every song-bird shout awhile for her;
But we are gifted, even in November
Rawest of seasons, with so huge a sense
Of her nakedly worn magnificence
We forget cruelty and past betrayal,
Heedless of where the next bright bolt may fall.

The Song of Blodeuwedd

(from the mediaeval Welsh)

Not of father nor of mother
Was my blood, was my body.
I was spellbound by Gwydion,
Prime enchanter of the Britons,
When he formed me from nine blossoms,
  Nine buds of various kind:
From primrose of the mountain,
Broom, meadow-sweet and cockle,
  Together intertwined,
From the bean in its shade bearing
A white spectral army
  Of earth, of earthy kind,
From blossoms of the nettle,
Oak, thorn and bashful chestnut –
Nine powers of nine flowers,
  Nine powers in me combined,
    Nine buds of plant and tree.
Long and white are my fingers
    As the ninth wave of the sea.

Instructions to the Orphic Adept

[In part translated from the Timpone Grande and
Campagno Orphic tablets.]

So soon as ever your mazed spirit descends
From daylight into darkness, Man, remember
What you have suffered here in Samothrace,
What you have suffered.

After your passage through Hell's seven floods,
Whose fumes of sulphur will have parched your throat,
The Halls of Judgement shall loom up before you,
A miracle of jasper and of onyx.
To the left hand there bubbles a black spring
Overshadowed with a great white cypress.
Avoid this spring, which is Forgetfulness;
Though all the common rout rush down to drink,
Avoid this spring.

To the right hand there lies a secret pool
Alive with speckled trout and fish of gold;
A hazel overshadows it. Ophion,
Primaeval serpent straggling in the branches,
Darts out his tongue. This holy pool is fed
By dripping water; guardians stand before it.
Run to this pool, the pool of Memory,
Run to this pool.

Then will the guardians scrutinize you, saying:
'Who are you, who? What have you to remember?
Do you not fear Ophion's flickering tongue?
Go rather to the spring beneath the cypress,
Flee from this pool.'

Then you shall answer: 'I am parched with thirst.
Give me to drink. I am a child of Earth,

But of Sky also, come from Samothrace.
Witness the glint of amber on my brow.
Out of the Pure I come, as you may see.
I also am of your thrice-blessed kin,
Child of the three-fold Queen of Samothrace;
Have made full quittance for my deeds of blood,
Have been by her invested in sea-purple,
And like a kid have fallen into milk,
Give me to drink, now I am parched with thirst,
Give me to drink!'

But they will ask you yet: 'What of your feet?'
You shall reply: 'My feet have borne me here
Out of the weary wheel, the circling years,
To that still, spokeless wheel:—Persephone.
Give me to drink!'

Then they will welcome you with fruit and flowers,
And lead you toward the ancient dripping hazel,
Crying: 'Brother of our immortal blood,
Drink and remember glorious Samothrace!'
Then you shall drink.

You shall drink deep of that refreshing draught,
To become lords of the uninitiated
Twittering ghosts, Hell's countless populace –
To become heroes, knights upon swift horses,
Pronouncing oracles from tall white tombs
By the nymphs tended. They with honey water
Shall pour libations to your serpent shapes,
That you may drink.

Lament for Pasiphaë

Dying sun, shine warm a little longer!
My eye, dazzled with tears, shall dazzle yours,
Conjuring you to shine and not to move.
You, sun, and I all afternoon have laboured
Beneath a dewless and oppressive cloud –
A fleece now gilded with our common grief
That this must be a night without a moon.
Dying sun, shine warm a little longer!

Faithless she was not: she was very woman,
Smiling with dire impartiality,
Sovereign, with heart unmatched, adored of men,
Until Spring's cuckoo with bedraggled plumes
Tempted her pity and her truth betrayed.
Then she who shone for all resigned her being,
And this must be a night without a moon.
Dying sun, shine warm a little longer!

Intercession in Late October

How hard the year dies; no frost yet.
On drifts of yellow sand Midas reclines,
Fearless of moaning reed or sullen wave.
Firm and fragrant still the brambleberries.
On ivy-bloom butterflies wag.

Spare him a little longer, Crone,
For his clean hands and love-submissive heart.

Counting the Beats

You, love, and I,
(He whispers) you and I,
And if no more than only you and I
What care you or I?

Counting the beats,
Counting the slow heart beats,
The bleeding to death of time in slow heart beats,
Wakeful they lie.

Cloudless day,
Night, and a cloudless day;
Yet the huge storm will burst upon their heads one day
From a bitter sky.

Where shall we be,

She whispers) where shall we be,
When death strikes home, O where then shall we be
Who were you and I?

Not there but here,
(He whispers) only here,
As we are, here, together, now and here,
Always you and I.

Counting the beats,
Counting the slow heart beats,
The bleeding to death of time in slow heart beats,
Wakeful they lie.

Your Private Way

Whether it was your way of walking
Or of laughing moved me,
At sight of you a song wavered
Ghostly on my lips; I could not voice it,
Uncertain what the notes or key.

Be thankful I am no musician,
Sweet Anonymity, to madden you
With your own private walking-laughing way
Imitated on a beggar's fiddle
Or blared across the square on All Fools' Day.

The Survivor

To die with a forlorn hope, but soon to be raised
By hags, the spoilers of the field, to elude their claws
And stand once more on a well-swept parade-ground,
Scarred and bemedalled, sword upright in fist
At head of a new undaunted company:

Is this joy? to be doubtless alive again,
And the others dead? Will your nostrils gladly savour
The fragrance, always new, of a first hedge-rose?
Will your ears be charmed by the thrush's melody
Sung as though he had himself devised it?

And is this joy: after the double suicide
(Heart against heart) to be restored entire,
To smooth your hair and wash away the life-blood,
And presently seek a young and innocent bride,
Whispering in the dark: 'for ever and ever'?

Questions in a Wood

The parson to his pallid spouse,
  The hangman to his whore,
Do both not mumble the same vows,
  Both knock at the same door?

And when the fury of their knocks
  Has waned, and that was that,
What answer comes, unless the pox
  Or one more parson's brat?

Tell me, my love, my flower of flowers,
  True woman to this man,
What have their deeds to do with ours
  Or any we might plan?

Your startled gaze, your restless hand,
  Your hair like Thames in flood,
And choked voice, battling to command
  The insurgence of your blood:

How can they spell the dark word said
  Ten thousand times a night
By women as corrupt and dead
  As you are proud and bright?

And how can I, in the same breath,
  Though warned against the cheat,
Vilely deliver love to death
  Wrapped in a rumpled sheet?

Yet, if from delicacy of pride
  We choose to hold apart,
Will no blue hag appear, to ride
  Hell's wager in each heart?

Darien

It is a poet's privilege and fate
To fall enamoured of the one Muse
Who variously haunts this island earth.

She was your mother, Darien,
And presaged by the darting halcyon bird
Would run green-sleeved along her ridges,
Treading the asphodels and heather-trees
With white feet bare.

Often at moonrise I had watched her go
And a cold shudder shook me
To see the curved blaze of her Cretan axe.
Averted her set face, her business
Not yet with me, long-striding,
She would ascend the peak and pass from sight.
But once at full moon, by the sea's verge,
I came upon her without warning.

Unrayed she stood, with long hair streaming,
A cockle-shell cupped in her warm hands,
Her axe propped idly on a stone.

No awe possessed me, only a great grief;
Wanly she smiled, but would not lift her eyes
(As a young girl will greet the stranger).
I stood upright, a head taller than she.
'See who has come,' said I.

She answered: 'If I lift my eyes to yours
And our eyes marry, man, what then?
Will they engender my son Darien?
Swifter than wind, with straight and nut-brown hair,
Tall, slender-shanked, grey-eyed, untameable;

Never was born, nor ever will be born
A child to equal my son Darien,
Guardian of the hid treasures of your world.'

I knew then by the trembling of her hands
For whom that flawless blade would sweep:
My own oracular head, swung by its hair.

'Mistress,' I cried, 'the times are evil
And you have charged me with their remedy.
O, where my head is now, let nothing be
But a clay counterfeit with nacre blink:
Only look up, so Darien may be born.

'He is the northern star, the spell of knowledge,
Pride of all hunters and all fishermen,
Your deathless fawn, an eaglet of your eyrie,
The topmost branch of your unfellable tree,
A tear streaking the summer night,
The new green of my hope.'
                                        Lifting her eyes,
She held mine for a lost eternity.
'Sweetheart,' said I, 'strike now, for Darien's sake!'

The Portrait

She speaks always in her own voice
Even to strangers; but those other women
Exercise their borrowed, or false, voices
Even on sons and daughters.

She can walk invisibly at noon
Along the high road; but those other women
Gleam phosphorescent – broad hips and gross fingers –
Down every lampless alley.

She is wild and innocent, pledged to love
Through all disaster; but those other women
Decry her for a witch or a common drab
And glare back when she greets them.

Here is her portrait, gazing sidelong at me,
The hair in disarray, the young eyes pleading:
'And you, love? As unlike those other men
As I those other women?'

Prometheus

Close bound in a familiar bed
All night I tossed, rolling my head;
Now dawn returns in vain, for still
The vulture squats on her warm hill.

I am in love as giants are
That dote upon the evening star,
And this lank bird is come to prove
The intractability of love.

Yet still, with greedy eye half shut,
Rend the raw liver from its gut:
Feed, jealousy, do not fly away –
If she who fetched you also stay.

The Straw

Peace, the wild valley streaked with torrents,
A hoopoe perched on his warm rock. Then why
This tremor of the straw between my fingers?

What should I fear? Have I not testimony
In her own hand, signed with her own name
That my love fell as lightning on her heart?

These questions, bird, are not rhetorical.
Watch how the straw twitches and leaps
As though the earth quaked at a distance.

Requited love; but better unrequited
If this chance instrument gives warning
Of cataclysmic anguish far away.

Were she at ease, warmed by the thought of me,
Would not my hand stay steady as this rock?
Have I undone her by my vehemence?

Dialogue on the Headland

SHE: You'll not forget these rocks and what I told you?
HE: How could I? Never: whatever happens.
SHE: What do you think might happen?
    Might you fall out of love? – did you mean that?
HE: Never, never! 'Whatever' was a sop
    For jealous listeners in the shadows.
SHE: You haven't answered me. I asked:
    'What do you think might happen?'
HE: Whatever happens: though the skies should fall
    Raining their larks and vultures in our laps –
SHE: 'Though the seas turn to slime' – say that –
    'Though water-snakes be hatched with six heads.'
HE: Though the seas turn to slime, or tower
    In an arching wave above us, three miles high –
SHE: 'Though she should break with you,' – dare you say
      that? –
    'Though she deny her words on oath.'
HE: I had that in my mind to say, or nearly;
    It hurt so much I choked it back.
SHE: How many other days can't you forget?
    How many other loves and landscapes?
HE: You are jealous?
SHE: Damnably.
HE: The past is past.
SHE: And this?
HE: Whatever happens, this goes on.
SHE: Without a future? Sweetheart, tell me now:
    What do you want of me? I must know that.
HE: Nothing that isn't freely mine already.
SHE: Say what is freely yours and you shall have it.
HE: Nothing that, loving you, I could dare take.
SHE: O, for an answer with no 'nothing' in it!
HE: Then give me everything that's left.

SHE: Left after what?

HE: After whatever happens:
Skies have already fallen, seas are slime,
Watersnakes poke and peer six-headedly –

SHE: And I lie snugly in the Devil's arms.

HE: I said: 'Whatever happens.' Are you crying?

SHE: You'll not forget me – ever, ever, ever?

The Mark

If, doubtful of your fate,
You seek to obliterate
And to forget
The counter-mark I set
In the warm blue-veined nook
Of your elbow crook,
How can you not repent
The experiment?

No knife nor fang went in
To lacerate the skin;
Nor may the eye
Tetter or wen descry:
The place which my lips pressed
Is coloured like the rest
And fed by the same blood
Of womanhood.

Acid, pumice-stone,
Lancings to the bone,
Would be in vain.
Here must the mark remain
As witness to such love
As nothing can remove
Or blur, or hide,
Save suicide.

The Sea Horse

Since now in every public place
Lurk phantoms who assume your walk and face,
You cannot yet have utterly abjured me
Nor stifled the insistent roar of the sea.

Do as I do: confide your unquiet love
(For one who never owed you less than love)
To this indomitable hippocamp,
Child of your element, coiled a-ramp,
Having ridden out worse tempests than you know of;
Under his horny ribs a blood-red stain
Portends the renewal of our pain.
Sweetheart, make much of him and shed
Tears on his taciturn dry head.

Dethronement

With pain pressing so close about your heart,
Stand (it behoves you), head uncovered,
To watch how she enacts her transformations –
Bitch, vixen, sow – the laughing, naked queen
Who has now dethroned you.

Hymns to her beauty or to her mercy
Would be ill-conceived. Your true anguish
Is all that she requires. You, turned to stone,
May not speak nor groan, shall stare dumbly.
Grinning dismay.

But as the play ends, or in its after-hush,
O then, deluded, flee! Her red-eared hounds
Scramble upon your track; past either cheek
Swan-feathered arrows whistle, or cruelly comb
Long furrows in your scalp.

Run, though you hope for nothing: to stay your foot
Would be ingratitude, a sour denial
That the life she bestowed was sweet.
Therefore be fleet, run gasping, draw the chase
Up the grand defile.

They will rend you to rags assuredly
With half a hundred love-bites –
Your hot blood an acceptable libation
Poured to Persephone, in whose domain
You shall again find peace.

Cat-Goddesses

A perverse habit of cat-goddesses –
Even the blackest of them, black as coals
Save for a new moon blazing on each breast,
With coral tongues and beryl eyes like lamps,
Long-leggèd, pacing three by three in nines –
This obstinate habit is to yield themselves,
In verisimilar love-ecstasies,
To tatter-eared and slinking alley-toms
No less below the common run of cats
Than they above it; which they do for spite,
To provoke jealousy – not the least abashed
By such gross-headed, rabbit-coloured litters
As soon as they shall be happy to desert.

The Blue-Fly

Five summer days, five summer nights,
The ignorant, loutish, giddy blue-fly
Hung without motion on the cling peach,
Humming occasionally: 'O my love, my fair one!'
     As in the *Canticles*.

Magnified one thousand times, the insect
Looks farcically human; laugh if you will!
Bald head, stage-fairy wings, blear eyes,
A caved-in chest, hairy black mandibles,
     Long spindly thighs.

The crime was detected on the sixth day.
What then could be said or done? By anyone?
It would have been vindictive, mean and what-not
To swat that fly for being a blue-fly,
     For debauch of a peach.

Is it fair, either, to bring a microscope
To bear on the case, even in search of truth?
Nature, doubtless, has some compelling cause
To glut the carriers of her epidemics –
     Nor did the peach complain.

A Lost Jewel

Who on your breast pillows his head now,
Jubilant to have won
The heart beneath on fire for him alone,

At dawn will hear you, plagued by nightmare,
Mumble and weep
About some blue jewel you were sworn to keep.

Wake, blink, laugh out in reassurance,
Yet your tears will say:
'It was not mine to lose or give away.

'For love it shone – never for the madness
Of a strange bed –
Light on my finger, fortune in my head.'

Roused by your naked grief and beauty,
For lust he will burn:
'Turn to me, sweetheart! Why do you not turn?'

The Window Sill

Presage and caveat not only seem
To come in dream,
But do so come in dream.

When the cock crew and phantoms floated by,
This dreamer I
Out of the house went I,

Down long unsteady streets to a queer square;
And who was there,
Or whom did I know there?

Julia, leaning on her window sill.
'I love you still,'
Said she, 'O love me still!'

I answered: 'Julia, do you love me best?'
'What of this breast,'
She mourned, 'this flowery breast?'

Then a wild sobbing spread from door to door,
And every floor
Cried shame on every floor,

As she unlaced her bosom to disclose
Each breast a rose,
A white and cankered rose.

Spoils

When all is over and you march for home,
The spoils of war are easily disposed of:
Standards, weapons of combat, helmets, drums
May decorate a staircase or a study,
While lesser gleanings of the battlefield –
Coins, watches, wedding-rings, gold teeth and such –
Are sold anonymously for solid cash.

The spoils of love present a different case,
When all is over and you march for home:
That lock of hair, these letters and the portrait
May not be publicly displayed; nor sold;
Nor burned; nor returned (the heart being obstinate) –
Yet never dare entrust them to a safe
For fear they burn a hole through two-foot steel.

Rhea

On her shut lids the lightning flickers,
Thunder explodes above her bed,
An inch from her lax arm the rain hisses;
Discrete she lies,

Not dead but entranced, dreamlessly
With slow breathing, her lips curved
In a half-smile archaic, her breast bare,
Hair astream.

The house rocks, a flood suddenly rising
Bears away bridges: oak and ash
Are shivered to the roots – royal green timber.
She nothing cares.

(Divine Augustus, trembling at the storm,
Wrapped sealskin on his thumb; divine Gaius
Made haste to hide himself in a deep cellar,
Distraught by fear.)

Rain, thunder, lightning: pretty children.
'Let them play,' her mother-mind repeats;
'They do no harm, unless from high spirits
Or by mishap.'

Leaving the Rest Unsaid

Finis, apparent on an earlier page,
With fallen obelisk for colophon,
Must this be here repeated?

Death has been ruefully announced
And to die once is death enough,
Be sure, for any life-time.

Must the book end, as you would end it,
With testamentary appendices
And graveyard indices?

But no, I will not lay me down
To let your tearful music mar
The decent mystery of my progress.

So now, my solemn ones, leaving the rest unsaid,
Rising in air as on a gander's wing
At a careless comma,

Index of First Lines

*Other books by Robert Graves
available in Penguins
are described on the
following pages*